Pathways to Joy

KAYANN ENGLEMAN

Olympus Story House

Contents

DAY 1 How Did We Get Here? 1

DAY 2 Repentance 4

DAY 3 Praying the Scriptures 7

DAY 4 Trust and Faith 11

DAY 5 Praise, Worship, and Thanksgiving 15

DAY 6 Proclaim and Declare 18

DAY 7 How Has Your Faith Grown 21

DAY 8 Pressing On 24

DAY 9 Repentance 28

DAY 10 Praying the Scriptures 31

DAY 11 Trust and Faith 35

DAY 12 Praise Worship and Thanksgiving 38

DAY 13 Proclaim and Declare 41

DAY 14 How Has Your Faith Grown 45

DAY 15 Pressing On 48

DAY 16 Repentance 51

DAY 17 Praying the Scriptures 54

DAY 18 Trust and Faith 57

DAY 19 Praise Worship and Thanksgiving 60

DAY 20 Proclaim and Declare 64

DAY 21 How Has Your Faith Grown 67

DAY 22 For the Sake of Joy 71

DAY 23 Repentance 74

DAY 24 Praying the Scriptures 77

DAY 25 Trust and Faith 81

DAY 26 Praise, Worship, and Thanksgiving 84

DAY 27 Proclaim and Declares 87

DAY 28 My, How Your Faith has Grown! 90

ABOUT THE AUTHOR 94

This book is to help guide you on a better path. Many of the stories you will read come through my own life experiences. Every person has a story but some have a book of Job story. I am a Job. My hope in writing "Pathways to Joy" is to walk alongside of you, to encourage you until you get to the other side. This life is not an easy journey, the Lord never promised that it would be. But it does become do-able when there is another walking along with you.

Writing "Pathways to joy" is the best way I can find to connect with you, hoping you will find me. You are worth my time and effort. Hold on. Be brave. Let us walk together by keeping your journey going forward.

I do not pretend to know it all, but all that I do know, I will do my best to pass on to you. I pray that your faith and trust in Jesus Christ, our Messiah, grows as you push through. Extend yourself grace and mercy as you work through the trails and testings you are going through with patient endurance. Above all, please, don't give up. You are going to make it. You are amazing!

DAY 1

How Did We Get Here?

Discouragement can come upon us through a means of something taking place that didn't go as planned, events taking place completely out of our control or not walking uprightly in our faith.

As a family, we opened up a business of organic, Non-GMO whole foods. We tried out our little business in a farmers' market first to see if it was what our community wanted. They did! Our customers wanted us to be open all the days in a week instead of just weekends. We found a storefront shop, signed a contract and opened the doors in April of that year.

By June our business was growing but I noticed I that labels were popping off our items. Droplets of water covered our cooler doors. Our wooden wall made of doors was warping and breaking away from each other. I got pretty sick with pneumonia. Next, we noticed it was getting warmer outside and inside. After setting up a humidity reader, we saw it was registering ninety percent humidity. We complained to the landlord that something seemed off with the air-conditioning.

His fairly new system was too big for our little space and moisture was being pumped in and not out. It was a $35,000.00 fix that he didn't want to do. In one month, we lost $11,000.00 of organic food in a business that had just open only a few months prior. We had to break the leasing contract and move in order to salvage.

That decision meant that the landlord could sue us for breaking the leasing contract. But if we stayed, my health was in jeopardy. He would not release us from the lease, so we had to leave. Within weeks, they handed court papers to us saying we were being sued for $50,000.00 for breech of rental contract. We found ourselves a lawyer. He explained that in our state, there is an enforced law against landlords who do not take care of mold issues and that we could sue the landlord for $100,000.00. That would be an automatic win for us with the proof we had. But it required an investigation and the fees that went with that investigation, lawyer fees, court fees and much stress to an already stressful situation and my health still hadn't fully recovered. The lawyer told us we could walk away with a battle that would take about 2 years to settle and if we were lucky, we would walk away with $35,000.00 after we paid all fees.

Our next option was to claim bankruptcy. Not because we couldn't pay our bills, but to stop all legal proceedings in their tracks. What? Bankrupt? Us? We have always been faithful to God. We honor Him in all that we do. Are we perfect? No! But, God, where are You? Why are you allowing all this to happen to us? This was a situation out of our control.

How did your discouragement came upon you?

_____

_____

_____

_____

_____

Were we angry? Yes, furious. We understood the cost of fixing the air-conditioning system was a decent chunk of money. But then to not release us from the lease, given we were a business of organic food, food without preservatives was cruel in my eyes. We couldn't bring anymore food into the store because it wouldn't last. Therefore, we couldn't make sales, leaving us to not pay bills all the way around. "God, where are You? Why won't You help us?"

Is that you? Have you had feelings that God has left you?

_____

_____

_____

_____

_____

For a time, I just couldn't pray. It felt like God checked out on me. I felt disconnected from people. It was a lonely battle of emotions, discouragement, anger, and feelings of failure.

What feelings and emotions are you experiencing?

_____

_____

_____

_____

_____

After deciding to declare bankruptcy, an instant calm came over us. The first bit of peace since everything started. Then God spoke to me, telling me we would not have to complete the five years of bankruptcy. It was a spark for my faith to be reignited.

You may or may not be at a place where your faith feels some life amid your own circumstance, but what can you say about the place you are in, and how would you rate your faith?

_____

_____

_____

_____

_____

2 Chronicles 15:7 "But as for you, be strong and courageous, for your work will be rewarded." NLT

DAY 2

Repentance

With all the injustice that happened during this difficult time, certain emotions took me on a down-ward spiral. I felt hurt over not feeling like God had control of this situation. I was Anger over the mistreatment from the landlord who did not get the air-conditioning system fixed. The stress from the whole thing caused our family relationships to suffer along with my marriage. I was becoming increasingly angry.

Another issue I faced was that it damaged my trust factor with people because of the lack of character from the landlord. Those trust issues flowed toward my faith in God for not doing something about the mess. Following trust issues with my family for turning against each other instead of pulling together to stand with each other and protecting each other.

There was a pure hate for all that happened. I was enjoying our store and the customers. I am a people person. Connecting with people through the store gave me a satisfaction that we were helping people become healthy. Now I needed help and our only option was bankruptcy. Why was this happening to us?

Have you asked, "Why me?" How were you answered?

_____

_____

_____

_____

_____

_____

Did you experience the same emotions that I experienced? What was it like for you?

_____

_____

_____

_____

_____

If you did not experience the same emotions as I have, write about the emotions you have experienced.

_____

_____

_____

_____

_____

_____

For me to even begin moving forward and become healed in my heart, I had to look at these emotions. Emotions in and of themselves are not a negative thing. They let us know that something is out of order, something that we do not agree with. But when we live off negative emotions and they become our constant companion, then there is a problem. We are stuck in our hurt. Repentance is a beginning point to get unstuck. Repentance begins with confession.

1 John 1:9 "But if we confess our sins to him, he is faithful and just to forgive us our sins and to cleanse us from all wickedness." NLT

Father God, I confess my hurt and angry with the landlord. Also, my hurt and anger towards my family and my husband, feelings of hurt and anger with You. I understand that Your ways are perfect and that all things work together for good. I don't understand why all this had to happen, but I want to grow and get past it. My trust took a big hit regarding You, and my family. I dislike how I am feeling right now, and I want to heal from it all. Humbled I come. Please forgive me and help me get through this trial. I long for my soul to be restored. Amen.

I want you to pray and confess for the healing to begin in your heart.

_____

_____

_____

_____

_____

To Repent means to walk away from, turn your back to. When we confess, we acknowledge our sin. When we repent, we are saying, "I am taking full responsibility for my actions and my sin and I am making the choice to never do this sin again." Repentance is not always easy, but it is necessary in order for the Lord to heal your wounded heart.

It is also important to voice our thoughts with the people who knowingly or unknowingly hurt us. I want you to be totally honest with your thoughts. Write freely the things you would like to say to those involved, even if that person is you.

_____

_____

_____

_____

_____

_____

_____

_____

Proverbs 28:13 "He who conceals his transgressions will not prosper, But whoever confesses and turns away from his sins will find compassion and mercy." AMP

DAY 3

Praying the Scriptures

Two of the best ways to overcome the thoughts and feelings you are going through are scripture and prayer. Speaking the scripture out loud and even praying out loud helps you to feel heard and understood. In Genesis, when God was creating the earth and everything in it, scripture says, "God said". Another example is when Christ Jesus was in the wilderness and the devil tempted Him, Jesus fought back by speaking scripture saying, "For it is written". There is creative power speaking the Word of God. Since we are made in the image of the Father and He is the one who gave us authority over everything, then it seems we should be like the Father and speak as He did and as Jesus did.

1 Peter 5:7 "Cast all your anxiety on Him because he cares for you." NIV

Father God, everything that is happening is very painful. How did I get into this place? I can't see an end in sight and now to know that we are going to file for bankruptcy, that too will be over our heads for at least 5 years. Will this ever end? But God! You spoke to me saying that it would not last the 5 years. I believe You. This bit of hope is enough for me to say, "Take this anxiety and fear Lord, I give it to you. I'm done with the sleepless nights and the consuming thoughts of trying to figure it all out. I need peace, Your peace, to consume me". Your scripture says that You care for me. Help me trust You. To know Father, You care for me and You will turn this horrible situation around. Amen.

What is your prayer for casting your anxiety on Him?

_____

_____

_____

_____

_____

_____

_____

James 1:4 "And let endurance have its perfect result and do a thorough work, so that you may be perfect and completely developed [in your faith], lacking in nothing." AMP

Father God, endurance is what You want from me. I don't feel strong enough to endure anymore. This whole thing has taken a toll on me. Help me, Lord. I am asking You to give me endurance. It is the work that You are doing in me I want. Quitting is not in my vocabulary, but right now that is where I am at. Can you do anything good with this mess? Your Word promises that if we will put our trust in You, then You will be faithful to bring good out of the bad. Father, God, not my will be done, but Your will be done. Amen.

Pray to the Father and ask Him to give you endurance so that you are lacking nothing.

_____

_____

_____

_____

_____

_____

_____

_____

The Father is not expecting perfection from us. He is looking for a willing heart. Do not let the devil beat you up with thoughts of failing God, added to the discouragement you are already facing. These trails we go through, no matter how they began, are to do a work of growth in us. They cause us to become more like Jesus.

As difficult as it is to face trials, we must look at them as opportunities for this growth that God is working in us. It only defeats us when we get our eyes off Jesus and on our troubles. The battle is in the mind. If we can take our thoughts captive and use the scripture to stand strong, the length of our battles or trails might end sooner. God will not let up till we get the very thing He is trying to teach us. A better way to describe this teaching is to call it "equipping us".

What the Lord was working in me during my discouragement was trust. I have always trusted God. But when a battle of this magnitude hit, my trust seemed none existent. How could this be? Even my friends questioned what was going on with me. How and why did trust feel so low? I would tell myself, "KayAnn, it isn't about big trust. It is about trust and faith the size of a mustard seed. That is it! I would then ponder the size of that seed. So small, yet it was enough for God. I thank the Lord that He will never ask of us for something that we can not do. With God, all things are possible, All Things!

Where do you need to see the possibility with the faith of the size of a mustard seed?

_____
_____
_____
_____
_____
_____
_____
_____
_____

Father, I pray for my brother/sister working with me to get through their trail. Be with them. Give them the strength and courage to keep moving forward. When they feel stuck, show them that all they need to do is ask You to help them take the next step. Show them that the situation is not impossible. If we have You nothing is impossible. Let them feel Your presence to know that they are not alone, for You promise to never leave us or forsake us. Please be ever close and present as they walk with You through to the other side of this difficult time. Amen.

1 Corinthians 10:13 "No test or temptation that comes your way is beyond the course of what others have had to face. All you need to remember is that God will never let you down; he'll never let you be pushed past your limit; he'll always be there to help you come through it." MSG

DAY 4

Trust and Faith

Losing our store, being served with a lawsuit, getting a lawyer who felt the best thing was bankruptcy, happened in months of us opening our store front. Being that everything took place so fast; I believe that is why I began having trust issues. I believed and still believe God wants us to prosper. When you believe God is good all the time, it is a contrary belief to think that He was not good in this situation. My thoughts turned to believing that I must have done something bad to cause such a dirty deal to happen to us. I began repenting of everything and anything I could think of. Perhaps I didn't read my Bible enough? Maybe I didn't pray enough?

This is all wrong thinking. These kinds of thoughts get us wrapped up in a works mentality. Meaning that only God will be good if we are good. That totally removes God's love, mercy, and grace from the "free" gifts that they are.

2 Corinthians 1:4 "He comforts us in all our troubles so that we can comfort others. When they are troubled, we will be able to give them the same comfort God has given us." NLT

Psalms 23:4 "Even when I walk through the darkest valley, I will not be afraid, for You are close beside me. Your rod and Your staff protect and comfort me." NLT

Notice these two scriptures talk of troubles and the darkest valley. We could never know the love, mercy, and grace of God if we never went through trials. We would never understand that He rescues, delivers, and gives victory if that is all we ever lived. Our spiritual growth would never happen. Do you understand this?

It is the same lesson if you are competing in an event. You would never understand the greatness of victories and receiving a trophy had you not first experienced defeat. Through our troubles, we are learning what it will take to help one another. You will not stay in the darkest valley. You will walk THROUGH dark valleys!

Do you feel God's presence walking with you? In what way?

_____

_____

_____

_____

_____

_____

_____

Psalm 37:5 "Commit your way to the Lord, Trust also in Him, And He shall bring it to pass." NKJV

We are not staying in our troubles. The Lord will bring it to pass. This is a promise. He told me it would not take five years till the bankruptcy would be over. I would hold on to that promise from Him till I saw it come to pass.

Hebrews 11:1 "Now faith is the substance of things hoped for, the evidence of things not seen." NKJV

In this verse, it is saying that faith is the thing we need to have hope in. And we need this hope in something that is not yet seen. If you have what you are hoping for, then you do not need faith because you already got it. But faith is for what we do not see. It is for what we do not yet have. Once the Lord provides it to you, you will no longer need to have faith in it. What you will have is a growth in faith for future troubles and dark valleys. He is faithful to you. His love compels Him to meet your needs.

Is hope starting to come to life in you?

_____

_____

_____

_____

_____

_____

_____

I don't expect that there is much change, but a sparkle of hope should cause a little light to get through these days of trouble and discouragement.

If you feel that your trust and faith are not enough, then ask the Lord to increase your measure of faith. For it is written in Romans 12:3 "For I say, through the grace given to me, to everyone who is among you, not to think of himself more highly than he ought to think, but to think soberly, as God has dealt to each one a measure of faith." NKJV God has given to each person a measure of faith. He wants our faith to grow. And it is through trials and testings that faith and trust get rooted and grounded in us. It is where our growth takes place. In this place, we look at the Lord and say I can't, but You can. This is trust and faith in action.

Can you think of a time where you had to trust that God would bring you through the thing you were going through? Write about that moment.

_____

_____

_____

_____

_____

_____

_____

Father, I pray You will cause my brother/sister to remember the times that You had brought them through difficulties. Times that seemed impossible, but You alone made a way through the impossible circumstances to "possible" circumstances. Show my brother/sister that You will be faithful even in this place of discouragement. Thank You, Father, for having control of their circumstances. I know You will turn this thing around for them. In Jesus', Name. Amen.

Romans 10:11 "For the scripture saith, Whosoever believeth on him shall not be ashamed." KJV

DAY 5

Praise, Worship, and Thanksgiving

One of the hardest things to do when we are hurting is to Praise God, and to worship Him offering thanksgiving to Him. Being able to praise, worship and offer thanksgiving shows that we are trusting Him. If we truly have given our discouragement over to Him, then we can worship Him with praise and thanksgiving.

The most obvious story in the Bible comes from Paul and Silas:

Acts 16:22-34 NLT "A mob quickly formed against Paul and Silas, and the city officials ordered them stripped and beaten with wooden rods. They were severely beaten, and then they were thrown into prison. The jailer was ordered to make sure they didn't escape. The jailer put them into the inner dungeon and clamped their feet in the stocks.

Around midnight, Paul and Silas were praying and singing hymns to God, and the other prisoners were listening. Suddenly, there was a massive earthquake, and the prison was shaken to its foundations. All the doors immediately flew open, and the chains of every prisoner fell off! The jailer woke up to see the prison doors wide open. He assumed the prisoners had escaped, so he drew his sword to kill himself. But Paul shouted to him, "Stop! Don't kill yourself! We are all here!"

The jailer called for lights and ran to the dungeon and fell down trembling before Paul and Silas. Then he brought them out and asked, "Sirs, what must I do to be saved?"

They replied, "Believe in the Lord Jesus and you will be saved, along with everyone in your household." And they shared the word of the Lord with him and with all who lived in his household. Even at that hour of the night, the jailer cared for them and washed their wounds. Then he and everyone in his household were immediately baptized. He brought them into his house and set a meal before them, and he and his entire household rejoiced because they all believed in God."

This example of worship in Acts not only shows Paul and Silas's trust in God during dark times, but in their trust, they became free, leading the jailer and his entire household to salvation. Their worship empowered them. It did not empower their circumstances. This is where God wants us to stand.

We read Paul, and Silas had been severely beaten. I question how they could have even stood in those shackles after such a beating. Yet it was that jailer who would care for their wounds. I can not even comprehend such faith. But I know concerning me the moment I stood up and pace my living room floor worshipping the Lord God Almighty, something broke in the spirit realm. My troubles still existed, but the oppression lifted, and the Lord got my purest form of worship. It was an amazing moment.

Praise God, thank Him for everything you can think of.

_____
_____
_____
_____
_____
_____
_____
_____
_____

I have given you room to pour out your worship. Go beyond the space I have given you. The Lord is worth it all, all that you can offer up to Him. Make this moment all about Him. Don't let the devil take this moment from you. The devil wants more than anything to take your mind off of God. Push through! Go for it and make this moment big for Jesus!

Write about this moment. Express how it made you feel.

_____
_____
_____
_____
_____

If you could not connect deeply with the Lord, it's ok. You gave it effort, and that is what God is looking for. When discouragement takes over, it takes time to disconnect from it and reconnect to God. Don't give up. Keep trying and putting forth your best effort. You're going to get there. I believe it, because I am praying for you.

The Lord will not let you go. He created you for a reason and as long as there is breath in you; the plan will come to fulfillment. He will keep bringing us to the same lesson till it causes us to grow. May we get it the first time around! Join with me in wanting to be a quick learner. Personally, I do not want to go through something difficult any longer than is necessary.

What about you? If you could tell the Lord to hurry things along but to not miss anything that you need to learn, what would you tell Him?

_____
_____
_____
_____
_____
_____
_____
_____
_____

Philippians 1:6 "I am sure of this very thing—that He who began a good work in you will carry it on to completion until the Day of Messiah Yeshua." TLV

DAY 6

Proclaim and Declare

The words that we speak are powerful. We have already discussed that the Father spoke and created everything through His spoken word. We also discussed how Jesus fought the devil in the wilderness by proclaiming "for it is written" in the scriptures.

Hebrews tells us just how powerful the Word of God is:

Hebrews 4:12 NKJV "For the word of God is living and powerful, and sharper than any two-edged sword, piercing even to the division of soul and spirit, and of joints and marrow, and is a discerner of the thoughts and intents of the heart."

Whenever you speak out loud the Word of God, you are speaking out life and power. The Word discerns the intent of the heart. If you are speaking out the Word of God, you are showing faith and trust in the power of that word. The Word of God is not a magic genie. It is taking it to a faith value. It is a mindset that says, "I believe what is written and that the Holy Spirit inspires the Word of God and everything written in it is yes and Amen!"

The Word of God tells us many times over that we will go through difficulties. But it also says that He will rescue us and bring us through it all. We cannot pick what we will believe concerning what is in the Word of God. Determine in your heart that you are going to stand on every single word that is written in the scriptures. This will empower you and you will walk in the authority that the Lord has established for us to walk in.

Let us look at these two scriptures and stand firm. From them, I will write a declaration and then proclaim that declaration out loud.

18

1 Corinthians 15:58 "Therefore, my beloved brothers and sisters, be steadfast, immovable, always excelling in the work of the Lord [always doing your best and doing more than is needed], being continually aware that your labor [even to the point of exhaustion] in the Lord is not futile nor wasted [it is never without purpose]." AMP

James 1:2-4 "Consider it nothing but joy, my brothers and sisters, whenever you fall into various trials. Be assured that the testing of your faith [through experience] produces endurance [leading to spiritual maturity, and inner peace]. And let endurance have its perfect result and do a thorough work, so that you may be perfect and completely developed [in your faith], lacking in nothing." AMP

Father, as Your daughter who was bought by the blood of Jesus, I will remain steadfast and immovable. I will continue to move forward in everything You have for me to do. I will not let discouragement take over my soul. What I am going through is painful, but I will keep my focus on what my trial will produce. It will perfect me in endurance, not lacking any part of it because I yield my soul to Your Holy Spirit. My flesh is weak and wants to take control of my emotions, but I will put all my trust in You, Lord, to complete the good work You are doing in me. I will waste none of what I am going through on self-pity. It is by my willingness and being yielded to You I will grow in faith and trust to have a deeper love for You. Thank You, Lord, for the full and completed work You are doing in me. So be it!

You can use these two scriptures to write your declaration, or you can use the scripture that really speaks to you. Write your declaration.

_____

_____

_____

_____

_____

_____

_____

_____

When I started proclaiming and declaring, I have to tell you, I really didn't feel like doing it. I was hurting and angry, and my flesh felt that it had a right to feel this way. The first thing I want to say to you is that proclaiming doesn't take away from the fact that something happened to you out of your control, but it gives you the power to not have that thing control you. Once it controls you, the fight to get over it will take much longer. And it will be harder to overcome.

I tell people you have three seconds to get rid of an ungodly thought or bad attitude before it puts a hook in your soul and takes you on a downward spiral. That is exactly what the devil wants you to do so that he can bind you up and take you captive in anger, bitterness, resentfulness, self-hatred, shame, etc... this list is never-ending. It is a sad thing to fall into the hands of the enemy whose plan is to destroy you.

There were days I was so down and could not find the strength to fight. After making a few calls, I asked friends to pray with me. I even asked if they would come to my house because I was weak from the battle and needed encouragement. I take a strong stand in having others surround you to help fight the battle. The Lord is about family. He calls us sons and daughters. When Jesus was training the disciples, He sent them out in twos. I have even told people when God was giving instructions to Noah about the ark; He had Noah put two of every kind of animal on the ark. Even the animals went in two by two.

There were times I could not connect with people. I knew God was doing this lesson between Him and me. It was a deep work that others could not understand. I cried in those moments from the depth of my being. At the right time, the healing came.

Luke 21:19 "For if you stand firm, you will win your souls." TLB

DAY 7

How Has Your Faith Grown

The purpose of going through difficulties is to grow spiritually. In seven days of working through Pathways to Joy, you may feel, at the very least, a spark of hope. My expectation for you is that you will take the things learned in these seven days and put them into practice.

A bodybuilder does not witness a change in their muscle tone after only a week. But they keep up the routine day after day, and in time, the changes will come to their muscle structure. They too must be patient and build endurance. Paul understood this concept when he wrote in, 1 Corinthians 9:27 "But [like a boxer] I strictly discipline my body and make it my slave, so that, after I have preached [the gospel] to others, I myself will not somehow be disqualified [as unfit for service]." AMP

You have the power and the authority to tell your flesh to be quiet. Paul said, "I strictly discipline my body." Paul made the choice to discipline himself. You can make the same decision. It is the flesh that we are working to overcome. Once we commit ourselves to Jesus, we become born of the spirit. Your spirit man comes alive. But because we are in this world born of our mothers, we still have to deal with the flesh, that perishable side of us.

The flesh wants us to fulfill the lusts (desires) of what it wants, but salvation is a walk that denies the lusts and seeks the things of God. Christ Jesus wants us to recognize our thoughts and feelings, but He does not want us to live off them. Thoughts and feelings can be deceiving.

Here is an example: Early in our marriage, I had an argument with my husband. He could not understand what I was trying to say. It caused me to feel unloved by him. I withdrew for a while to cry and get over the emotion of rejection I was experiencing. I did not go to him to deal with the emotion because I felt that his lack of understanding would cause more pain. This put up a wall between us that he didn't understand. The day came when the wall was getting thicker, and he was done with feeling cut off. I went back to the day we had the argument and explained to him it made me feel unloved. This caused him to feel hurt that I didn't come to him sooner to explain what I was going through.

So many times, my feelings would deceive me, causing me to feel unloved. Time would teach me that as soon as I feel something that seemed contrary to what should be the truth, I needed to address it right away. I needed to tell my feelings, "Be quiet! I don't trust you. It feels like you have deceived me too many times. I'd tell the Lord, "Lord, lead me into all truth. Help me go in love with my husband and discuss the hurt openly and honestly."

Weeks went by that I lived feeling unloved, weeks that the devil held me in captivity. That actually caused more pain than had I dealt with things from the get go. If you will apply this week's lesson and disciple your mind, will, and emotions, you will be on your way to living a victorious Christian life. People will watch you from a distance and see that you are different. They will ask how are you getting through what you're going through. This opens the door to sharing your testimony. That is what this lesson is all about, overcoming and growing spiritually to where you can now help others get through the discouragement they are going through.

We all need to hear God speak to us. His desire is to speak with us. I have journaled for many years. I have learned the art of sitting quietly with my journal and pen, waiting on God to speak into my thoughts. This is my favorite time of the day. I have taught others to journal using the question below. Like myself, they marvel at what they wrote. Taken note that, "This has to be from the Lord, because I would not say these things to myself." This becomes a powerful tool for us to connect with the Lord.

Answer this question: What do you need to hear God say to you?

_____

_____

_____

_____

_____

_____

_____

_____

Cherish your writing. God is speaking to you. He knows what you need to hear. Never will He leave you. He is with you always. We just have to look for Him more intently and with purpose. We will discuss this more in the coming days.

Let us review: Determine where discouragement began. Repentance. Own what you did on your part that does not line up with the Word of God. See your trial as an opportunity for growth, not destruction. You will not stay in this place. You are going THROUGH this place. Praise, worship and thanksgiving are keys to getting through in a more timely manner. Speak life! You have 3 seconds to get rid of a negative thought.

Heavenly Father, I thank you for this week spent with my brother/ sister. It is difficulties that have brought us together and it will be victory through Jesus that keeps us family. I pray that as they work through the discouragement going on inside of them, that You will give them spiritual strength. I know You are proud of my brother/sister for all the effort they are putting forth to overcome. Let Your presence devotedly give them the strength and encouragement to complete this Pathway to Joy. I know when discouragement had me weighed down that it was hard for me to see the light at the end of the tunnel. I hope that my brother/sister will gain from my experiences so that they too will lead those who are suffering to their victory, oh Faithful Lord. Amen.

Joshua 1:9 "Have I not commanded you? Be strong and of good courage; do not be afraid, nor be dismayed (intimidated), for the Lord your God is with you wherever you go." AMP

DAY 8

Pressing On

Now that we have a plan laid out for you that scripturally guides you out of discouragement and into joy, I want to take the rest of our time and go deeper into each of the categories. Through this journey of going deeper, it will take your will combined with passion and the leading of the Holy Spirit to guide you on the pathway He has designed for you.

If you want to walk in the will of God, you will have to surrender yourself to Him. This goes back to when we talked about Paul disciplining his body.

Are you finding it difficult to stand firm on God's word to overcome discouragement? Explain where you believe the problem lies.

_____
_____
_____
_____
_____
_____

Through genetic testing, I found out I am an HSP (Highly Sensitive Person) or the scientific name is SPS (Sensory Processing Sensitivity). Seventeen percent of the world's population is HSP. This causes me to feel deeply in my emotions. I love deeply and hurt deeply. I feel the good, bad and ugly of what others are feeling. When someone I know has come to the end of this life, that brings up very complex emotions for me.

To be in heaven is to be home. To see Jesus as He is. That thought alone makes me feel excited because I cannot wait for that day. On the other hand, the grief and loneliness I feel with their passing goes deep. I don't just know grief; I live it deeply. My emotions are powerful. I have to work at throwing my mental switch in the right direction or my emotions will be more than I can bear. They will overpower me if I let them.

It is the hardest thing for me to switch over in my brain how I'm going to choose to feel. This took time to learn. For a moment, I might have to get alone by myself to cry out my emotions first. If I can empty enough emotion out, then I have room to discipline my thought life. My constant prayer is asking God for strength to not let my emotions consume me. I am fully aware how much I need His help to do this. I have to shake myself off and stand firm in my decision. Now and then, I have to cry and let out emotions that might hinder my push to overcome. But whatever it takes, I am determined to keep going forward. I want more than anything to be in the place that God wants me in.

Do you allow yourself to have an emotional moment?

_____

_____

_____

_____

_____

_____

I have taught many times about tears. In our western culture, we view crying as weakness. I cannot even express how angry that makes me. God created us and everything about us. That means He created our tear ducts and the tears that flow out of them. Tears serve a spiritual purpose, as you can see from these scriptures.

Psalm 56:8 "You keep track of all my sorrows. You have collected all my tears in Your bottle. You have recorded each one in Your book." NLT

Job 16:20 "My friends scorn me, But I pour out my tears to God." NLT

Psalm 126:5 "Those who plant in tears will harvest with shouts of joy." NLT

Luke 7:38 "Then she knelt behind Him at His feet, weeping. Her tears fell on His feet, and she wiped them off with her hair. Then she kept kissing His feet and putting perfume on them." NLT

Give Him your tears. He wants to record and remember what each one represents. It is a strong, healthy person who yielded to the Lord that will let Him have their tears. Tears showing weakness is a lie that we have believed, and it has cost us a special place in the heart of God. Please release your tears to Him today.

What are your thoughts on tears?

_____

_____

_____

_____

_____

_____

When is the last time that you really cried? What brought you to tears?

_____

_____

_____

_____

_____

_____

I believe you want to draw closer to the Lord and become more than a conqueror. He will be the glory and the lifter of your head. Your Father in heaven is proud of you. The Word of God says that you are His delight. And He has done everything impossible to make possible a way for you to be free. Whom He sets free is free indeed. And your freedom is already awaiting you. You are going to make it because you got the greatest Love fighting with you. That is the love of a Father.

Isaiah 28:5-8 "He will swallow up death (and abolish it) for all time. And the Lord God will wipe away tears from all faces, and He will take away the disgrace of His people from all the earth; For the Lord has spoken." AMP

DAY 9

Repentance

One day while take a shower I noticed an earwig bug come out from under the shower curtain. Earwigs have a sharp pincher on their back end. When they punch is sends a zinger feeling through you and it hurts like a bee sting. I cupped my hands and filled them with water. Pouring the water over the earwig. I hoped to wash it down the drain. But that bug came crawling up out of the drain.

I attempted a second time to wash it down the drain. I waited. Then did the happy dance that it was gone. Finishing up my shower, I looked down and there was that earwig again coming out from under the curtains. I had this feel the Lord was trying to show me something. I prayed and asked the Lord what is the lesson I'm to learn from this bug?

He told me that the earwig was like an unrepentant heart. When sin is in our lives, it makes us feel uncomfortable. Instead of trying to pray and ask forgiveness, we want to sweep the uncomfortable away ourselves. We try to wash it down the drain. But the funny thing about sin is that it only goes away one way. That way is through the blood of Jesus and not a shower.

When we take water to wash stains away, it can leave traces of the stain behind. We need something that is more powerful than water. Something that will fully cover that stain. The only thing strong enough to wash over the stain of sin is the blood of Jesus. Just like putting paint on a wall. It is thick enough to cover over dirt and grime and look brand new. The blood of Jesus applies to the repented sin and makes you like new, white as snow with no spot of a sin stain. And that uncomfortable feeling is washed away with it. Without the blood, sin has the ability to keep coming at us and trying to pinch us with that stinger like feeling.

Describe how sin makes you feel.

_____

_____

_____

_____

_____

_____

How does sin make me feel? Honestly, sin makes me feel sick in my stomach. I just don't feel good. I feel uneasy with no rest or peace. Those feelings will exaggerate if it is a sin that Christ conquerored in my life and I somehow let it happen again. I am now quick to repent so that I don't feel sick from the sinning. Sin is always at my door and your door. There are times it gets me, but repenting as soon as I recognize it will keep me sensitive and alert from being caught off guard for the next time.

The Lord is not on His throne, ready to send out bolts of lightning to strike you down because of sin. He is gentle in His nudges of revealing sin. In Love the Lord uncovers our motives and with compassion leads us to repentance. It is for our health and our lives that God wants us free from sin. The next time you pray for repentance, think about the great level of love the Father has for you. He gave you His Son. Jesus, God's Son, was called to a cross that would stretch out His arms to carry the weight of your sin. He was also stretched out to receive you into those open arms of love. Repenting and trusting Jesus to clean up your soul is like saying, "I receive Your love for me. I can see how much You love me. I want to honor you and love you back by repenting of all sins I have committed against You. You are worth living in a clean temple. Wash me and cleanse me of all sin. In Jesus', Name. Amen"

You are the temple of the Holy Spirit. The Word of God says that He is in us and we are in Him. This is a sacred holy moment of love at such a deep level. So go deep. Remember, I said we would go deeper, but that deep place will require your willingness. The truth is, you will never regret going there. It is the very thing your soul is crying out for. Run! Do not walk. Our Father is waiting.

Negative words, unhealthy thoughts, anger, shame, fear of failure, lustful thoughts, jealousy, envy, selfishness, greed, gluttony. This is a list of common overlooked sins. Many of these sins are daily habits that God wants to rid our souls of. Is there anything on this list that you need to go before the Lord with? Or is the Father showing you something else?

_____

_____

_____

_____

_____

How does true repentance make you feel?

_____

_____

_____

_____

_____

Repenting will never bring the Lord's judgment on you. Repenting brings the favor of God to you. It shows you trust Him. It takes trust to be able to go to Him and admit your failures and mistakes. Nothing could please Him more that. A heart that yields to Him for cleansing.

I am proud of how you are hanging in there and pressing on to have a deeper relationship with the Lord. Being a Christian is difficult, but it is the only way to live. He is your help through all of life's circumstances. You can not do life without Him. I know He is with you right now and He wants the best for you. Stay strong, my friend, stay strong and full of hope. This lesson will not last forever, but the workout it is doing in you will last for eternity.

Zephaniah 3:17 "The Lord you God is in your midst, a Warrior who saves. He will rejoice over you with joy; He will be quiet in His love (making no mention of your past sins), He will rejoice over you with shouts of joy." AMP

DAY 10

Praying the Scriptures

Since the Word of God is full of life giving scripture, we are going to look at more scripture. To keep God's Word fresh in my spirit, I look for new scriptures. I always want His Word to remain powerful.

I am a part of a worship dance team. I have to be very careful when I am working on a song that I don't overdo it with practicing. The song will go from being inspiring to mundane. I'm a creative, artsy person. I love change. It keeps it fresh for me. If you are anything like my personality, then you will understand what I'm talking about. I fully understand that God made us all different. You may be good at the same meaningful scriptures and that is perfectly fine.

1 Corinthians 10:13 "No temptations has overtaken you except what is common to mankind. And God is faithful; He will not let you be tempted beyond what you can bear. But when you are tempted, He will also provide a way out so that you can endure it." NIV

Father, God, I am putting forth effort to give You all that I have. Help me walk in freedom and wholeness. I want to totally surrendered to Your will. Sometimes it just seems too hard and I want to quit. I have to really fight the urge to not give up. Your Word says that what I feel is common to others. I see I am not alone in these feelings. Since You are faithful, I am crying out for a way of escape. Help me stay strong and not give up. I need endurance. Be my strength. Thank You for giving

Your Word to me so that I can know what Your promises are. I trust Your Word. That brings me hope. Amen.

You may use the same scripture or find one that speaks more directly to your needs. With that scripture, write out your prayer based on that scripture's promise.

_____

_____

_____

_____

_____

You're doing good. God will not let you become lost, not when you are seeking His will for your life and through your difficult circumstances. He is right there with you. Some of our life lesson take more time than others to get to the end. Extend yourself patients. He will never let you fail.

There was a day when I just was not feeling I could fight to stay on top. Still broken over losing the business, I was once again battling sickness. I was in so much pain I could get out of bed. They were testing me for lupus, rheumatoid arthritis, and limes disease. Thank God all my blood work came back negative, but I was battling fear, not knowing why I was in so much pain. Discouragement was taking on a new level. Quickly I called two friends and said, "I need you today so much. I'm weak physically, emotional, and spiritual. I just can not fight today and I need a friend who will pray with me and help me get back into the fight." They both came. As I laid there, we talked, prayed, and laughed. I needed that laughter. I couldn't even remember when I had the chance to laugh. Though it didn't take the pain away, those two wonderful friends became a lifeline for me that day.

Who Is your life line? Have you felt free enough to call on your friends or family to fight with you?

_____

_____

_____

_____

_____

Job 8:12 "He will once again fill your mouth with laughter and your lips with shouts of joy." NLT

Proverbs 17:22 "A cheerful heart is good medicine, but a crushed spirit dries up the bones." NIV

John 15:11 "These things I have spoken to you so the My joy may be in you, and that joy Made be made full." NKJV

Write about a moment that brought you such joy.

_____
_____
_____
_____
_____
_____
_____

Father, I thank You, for You will once again bringing me laughter. You have also promised me I will shout for joy, too. I want this "good medicine," joy and laughter. Help me remember the past moments of joy. Cause my mind to remember! Please do not allow my present circumstance hide memories of the past. Let them be a hope and sign to me I am not staying in this place. Help me make wonderful new memories. Amen.

The Bible repeats the story of the children leaving Egypt and journeying through the wilderness many times. The reason for this repeating is for the people to remember. God delivered His people then and He will do it again. Remembering the good things the Lord has done throughout your life will keep hope alive. Remember my brother/ sister, remember! Make a list of things the Lord brought you through. Even think back on the days before you believed in Jesus and received salvation. What did He do in your life that you can see His hand was always on you?

Philippians 4:8 "Finally, brethren, whatever things are true, whatever things are noble, whatever things are just, whatever things are pure, whatever things are lovely, whatever things are of good report, if there is any virtue and if there is anything praiseworthy— meditate on these things." NKJV

DAY 11

Trust and Faith

Genesis 15:5-6 "Then he took him outside and said, "Look at the sky. Count the stars. Can you do it? Count your descendants! You're going to have a big family, Abram!" And he believed! Believed God! God declared him "Set-Right-with-God." MSG

God counted Abraham as righteous, for he believed what the Lord had spoken to him. Abraham had faith and trusted in the Lord. He believed! Can you count all your descendants all the way back to Abraham?

We have something Abraham did not have. We have a record of our descendants when we do the research. My sister recently studied our family line. She got as far back as the early 1600s. That is still not far enough back to get to Abraham's time era. So let me ask you, if you were Abraham and God just spoke to you that your descendants are the amount as the amount of stars in the sky, and you are an old childless man or woman would you have enough faith and trust in the Lord to believe it will be?

When we are seeking answers to our needs from the Lord, we are seeking Him to meet the needs that we do not have. That takes faith and trust on our part. Once the Lord meets the need, we no longer need faith for that thing, because we now have obtained it. But here is what that thing produces in us, a greater measure of faith. Now that we have the blessing of God who met our need, we will become quicker at trusting and having faith for future needs to be met because God showed Himself faithful.

The same is true when we turn to God and we have this expectation of how God should meet our needs and it does not meet with our expectation. We then look at God as not meeting our needs and our trust and faith in Him takes a nosedive. Sadly, this happened to me when we lost our business. None of what we went through turned out the way I thought it should. I felt let down by God. So when the next thing came along that I need to trust Him for, I struggled with giving it to the Lord.

Many who knew me found it hard that I struggled with trusting the Lord. They know I love Him with all my heart. He is and has always been my everything. I have countless stories about how God has always provided for every need. So why now? Why was I losing trust and faith?

There were too many things coming at me at one time. I felt like I couldn't come up for air. I was battling a sickness that I was told it was in my head or that it was caused by anxiety. Years later, they would diagnose me with Hashimoto Thyroiditis. Next, we had 14 people in our circle of friends and family die in four weeks. Shortly thereafter, we would also lose two of our dogs to cancer. Right before we lost our business, we were in a head on collision. It appears the other driver who hit us might have suffered a stroke while driving. This is just a part of the list. There is so much more. I call this time period my "Job" experience.

With all that was happening at the same time frame, I was sinking in discouragement. I remember crying out to God and telling Him I would never walk away from Him because I saw too much of His goodness. But all that has happened has rocked my faith. In that moment of despair, He spoke to my heart. He said, "KayAnn, I Am with you. I will never leave you nor forsake, NEVER!" I had to look that verse up in Hebrews, Greek, and the dictionary meanings and here is how it read when I put all those meanings together:

"Never will I Forsake you. Not ever, at no time, absolutely not, will I go out of or away from you. I will not quit or cease to exist concerning you. Never, at no time, absolutely not will I abandon, desert, or give up on you. Mentally powerful, vigorous and fearless, heroic, strong, tenacious, assured, lionhearted. Do not be afraid, for the Lord Himself goes earlier and in front of, ahead of, before, in the future of awaiting you. Don't be afraid." Taking from scriptures Deuteronomy 31:6,8 and also Hebrew 13:5.

I read this daily for a long time and I saw hope come back. I came to this place of understanding that I will not always understand God's ways, but He will never leave me. He goes ahead of me. And I will follow even if it is too dark to see the way. He is ahead of me.

Tell the Lord how you don't always understand everything you are going through, but with the amount of trust and faith you have at this moment, how you are going to hold on to Him.

_____

_____

_____

_____

_____

_____

_____

_____

_____

_____

Take a long, deep breath. Now release it. Do it again, and several more times. That breath you breathe goes into your lungs and is an ability that God gave you. Your very breath was from the Lord as He breathed into the nostrils of Adam and it has passed down to you. Receive the gift of the breath of life from the Father and allow yourself to breathe.

Isaiah 43:1-2 "But now thus saith the Lord that created thee, O Jacob, and he that formed thee, O Israel, Fear not: for I have redeemed thee, I have called thee by thy name; thou art mine. When thou passest through the waters, I will be with thee; and through the rivers, they shall not overflow thee: when thou walkest through the fire, thou shalt not be burned; neither shall the flame kindle upon thee." KJV

DAY 12

Praise Worship and Thanksgiving

In the early nineties, I learned the power of praise, worship, and thanksgiving. We had just started going to a church that was developing a dance team. I was so amazed by the flags and veils and the creative instruments of praise that I joined the team. I knew little about what they were doing or why they were doing it, but I had always wanted to dance since I was little, and that it was happening in church made it all the better. During this same time, my youngest son, who was only a year old, was fighting a pretty severe cold. He was not getting better, so I took him to the doctor. They instantly diagnosed him with pneumonia. Right there, in the office, they gave him a shot of antibiotics. They gave me instructions to call in four hours to let them know how he was progressing. If I didn't see any improvement, he would need to be transported to the hospital.

Once we got home, I took this sick little boy and put him in his crib. I sat on the floor in front of him, crying and asking the Lord to heal him. I heard the Lord speak to my heart, saying, "Get out your flag and worship Me." Putting his crib in the middle of the room, I put on worship music and danced around his crib and worshipped God. In one hour, his fever had broken. Within two hours, my son was sitting up in his crib. It was amazing. I called the doctor and told them the good news. It was the day I learned the value of worship.

Scripture says, "He inhabits the praises of his people" Psalm 22:3 (my paraphrase). That day, I did not focus on how sick my child was when I got up to dance around him. Somehow, I knew the Lord wanted me to worship Him despite my circumstances. I gave it my all, because He is so worthy of my praise. After the immediate changes in his condition, I thanked the Lord with tears of joy and gladness. It was a moment in time that God was showing me a part of His nature.

His nature wants us to praise and worship Him, no matter what is going on. The reason being that our circumstance will never, "no, not ever," be as big as He is. Since He is the only one who can change our circumstances, it seems fitting to just worship Him, anyway.

Hebrews 13:15-16 "Let us, then, always offer praise to God as our sacrifice through Jesus, which is the offering presented by lips that confess him as Lord. Do not forget to do good and to help one another, because these are the sacrifices that please God." GNT

Give Him your words of praise.

_____

_____

_____

_____

_____

_____

Romans 1:21 "For even though they knew God [as the Creator], they did not honor Him as God or give thanks for His wondrous creation. On the contrary, they became worthless in their thinking [godless, with pointless reasonings, and silly speculations], and their foolish heart was darkened." AMP

What would it have looked like if I had not worshipped Him that day? Stay strong in your praise and worship. Give him your thanksgiving even before you see your answers to your situations.

What can you thank the Lord for today?

_____

_____

_____

_____

One thing I did during this discouraging time of losing our business was to write in my journal everyday things I was grateful for. Some days, it felt like I was pulling thanksgiving out of thin air, because things were that bad. But I still made myself thank the Lord. From that lesson the Lord taught me concerning my son and his healing, the one thing I can thank the Lord for is the breath in my lungs. I thank Him for the song of praise in my head. I thank Him for eyes that see and the revelations He teaches me.

None of this is about us, it is all about Him. It always was and always will be. When we look at us and telling ourselves the "woo is me" song, that is when our trust and faith lose their strength to hold us up. I can never stop worshipping Him. I need His strength to make it through the day.

Jesus taught me through that dance team how to love Him with all I had. For a few years, in the beginning of being on the team, it seemed every time we got up to dance, I would have a panic attack. The team would prepare to go out and minister the number to the congregation and they would have to turn to me and pray for me to stop the panic. I didn't enjoy being up in front of people like that. But when I learned it wasn't

about me and all about Jesus, the panic stopped. I would see myself dancing with Jesus, not looking at the people but causing my spiritual eyes to see only Jesus. I danced for an audience of one, Jesus. He is my everything. Who do I dance for? I dance for my King of Kings and my Lord of Lords, the lover of my soul!

What can you do to give Him your praise, worship, and thanksgiving?

_____

_____

_____

_____

_____

DAY 13

Proclaim and Declare

Psalm 118:17 "I shall not die, but live, And declare the works of Jehovah." ASV

My Lord, there is NO death found in You, only life. Therefore, You have given me life because You live in me. This is good news to those that hear it. I will speak Your Good News for all to hear.

Luke 15:8-10 "Or imagine a woman who has ten coins and loses one. Won't she light a lamp and scour the house, looking in every nook and cranny until she finds it? And when she finds it you can be sure she'll call her friends and neighbors: 'Celebrate with me! I found my lost coin!' Count on it—that's the kind of party God's angels throw every time one lost soul turns to God." MSG

This story astonishes me. That this woman would call together her friends and neighbors to come celebrate with her over a coin that once lost but is now found! People celebrated over such things in Bible times. It was a reason for fellowship. She knew it was only by the grace of God that the coin had been found. We can do nothing without the Lord. The Lord loves when we get together to fellowship and rejoice, making it all about Him and His goodness.

I want you to take a step outside your box and have a fellowship party. I do not care about the number of people you invite. Invite one or five people. The numbers do not matter. But have a party where all you talk about is the things the Lord has done for each other. Don't talk about anything else, only what the Lord has done.

This pleases Him to be talked about in a praiseworthy manner. Your benefit is that it will stir up everyone's faith. It breaks off discouragement, even if it is just for a short time. It brings laughter, which is the merry heart, and that does good like medicine. In this next scripture, it is clear God loves when we speak, write, and declare the things that He has done for us.

1 John 1:3-4 "That which we have seen and heard declare we unto you also, that ye also may have fellowship with us: yea, and our fellowship is with the Father, and with his Son Jesus Christ: and these things we write, that our joy may be made full." ASV

This party may turn into a prayer meeting where everyone is praying for each other! Isn't this something you would want? It's ok to rejoice and declare that the Lord is good. It is also good to confess your need for prayer and have others pray for you, and you pray for them.

Matthew 18:20 "For where two or three are gathered together in my name, there am I in the midst of them." KJV

This may be a big step for some people, but for others, it is a straightforward thing to do. One thing is for sure: it would never displease the Lord. Who knows if it would speed up the process for taking your discouragement and turning it into joy and victory? It could even become a weekly thing or even a once a month thing. If you do not feel comfortable leading the group, find a person in your group who is. You will be the host and let another person be the facilitator. Or take turns letting each person lead, causing them to use their gifts and callings. As long as you keep the Lord the primary focus, this will not fail.

Make a list of who you will invite to your declaring the goodness of the Lord party.

Keep it simple. If you want to do food, ask everyone to bring a snack. Or just have a coffee or tea time. If you have a fireplace, light a fire. If it is warm outside and you can make an outdoor fire, do that. Maybe the best time is a Saturday morning. Figure out what will work for everyone and set the time and place.

Where will you meet?

Be casual and relaxed. You can do this. Just think about how much this will bless the Lord. He will have much delight in you and all who will join you.

Exodus 9:16 "But I have raised you up for this very purpose, that I might show you my power and that my name might be proclaimed in all the earth." NIV

Father, You are raising up my brother/sister to tell of Your good deeds. I believe You are doing good things in them to give them something to talk about. Father, bring the right people to this party who will fully declare and proclaim the goodness of God. I pray for the anointing of the Holy Spirit to touch all that attend and Your anointing would cause a manifestation of Your presence to be felt by everyone there. May this declaration party do a new thing in all their lives. May they all leave rejoicing in what You have done and are continuing to do to strengthen and heal each person there. In Jesus' Name. Amen.

Record highlights from your declaration party.

Psalm 35:18 "I will give you thanks in the great assembly; among the throngs I will praise you." NIV

DAY 14

How Has Your Faith Grown

It is a step by step, one day at a time, walk with the Lord. He is patient and long suffering. The Lord is with you as you embark on this journey to break the hold of discouragement off you. I believe you are growing in your faith and trust. I am encouraged by your willingness to walk through this process to healing. You doing a good job.

What has the Lord been showing you this past week?

_____

_____

_____

_____

_____

What do you need to hear the Lord speak to you?

_____

_____

_____

_____

Nobody knows you better than the One who created you. He knows exactly what you need and how to supply that need. There is this way about a Christian life that is so simple yet so complex. The things the Lord is bringing you through will help others get through similar situations. It will be your words of encouragement, extending mercy, and hope that will draw others to you. Seeing if you made it, then they will make it too. But what they will most likely not experience is the process the Lord took you through.

There are three-step programs out there. Even seven and ten step programs, but they are to be used only as a guide. We must let God lead and do it His way and in His time. The work He does in us is such a personal work. He perfectly designs each person's pathway as to not to leave nothing missing. Look with me at some verses and see how each incident is so different, yet they all lead to healing.

Luke 18:35-43 "And it came to pass, as he drew nigh unto Jericho, a certain blind man sat by the way side begging: and hearing a multitude going by, he inquired what this meant. And they told him, that Jesus of Nazareth passeth by. And he cried, saying, Jesus, thou son of David, have mercy on me. And they that went before rebuked him, that he should hold his peace: but he cried out the more a great deal, Thou son of David, have mercy on me. And Jesus stood, and commanded him to be brought unto him: and when he was come near, he asked him, What wilt thou that I should do unto thee? And he said, Lord, that I may receive my sight. And Jesus said unto him, Receive thy sight: thy faith hath made thee whole. And immediately he received his sight, and followed him, glorifying God: and all the people, when they saw it, gave praise unto God." ASV

John 9"1-7 "And as he passed by, he saw a man blind from his birth. And his disciples asked him, saying, Rabbi, who sinned, this man, or his parents, that he should be born blind? Jesus answered, Neither did this man sin, nor his parents: but that the works of God should be made manifest in him. We must work the works of him that sent me, while it is day: the night cometh, when no man can work. When I am in the world, I am the light of the world. When he had thus spoken, he spat on the ground, and made clay of the spittle, and anointed his eyes with the clay, and said unto him, Go, wash in the pool of Siloam (which is by interpretation, Sent). He went away therefore, and washed, and came seeing." ASV

Mark 8:22-25 "And they come unto Bethsaida. And they bring to him a blind man, and beseech him to touch him. And he took hold of the blind man by the hand, and brought him out of the village; and when he had spit on his eyes, and laid his hands upon him, he asked him, Seest thou aught? And he looked up, and said, I see men; for I behold them as trees, walking. Then again he laid his hands upon his eyes; and he looked stedfastly, and was restored, and saw all things clearly." ASV

This is the way of the Lord to not do things the same way. I believe that people are conditioned to looking for the easy fix. Speak and it will be, but that is not always the reality. Truth be told, it sure is exciting when that happens, but again, it is not the average way of the Lord. He is teaching us lessons when things are going on in our lives. How He is teaching and leading us through is so very different from each other.

I can present this book to the world on steps that you may take to help lead you toward healing, but ultimately it will be the Lord of Lords who orders your steps. We have to begin to take some kind of steps. The same is true as we try to help others go through what we have been through. We must encourage them and give them examples of our journey. We can not tell them exactly how to do it. We must leave that up to the Lord.

The Lord is holy, and He is doing a holy work in us. It is by His Holy Spirit that we will learn, heal, and move forward in life with strength and power as we grow. My brother/sister your are growing. You are becoming stronger. You are becoming a walking miracle for others to witness the power of God working in you and giving others faith to see that they will look like Jesus when the Lord has finished the work in them. Together, we are passing onward and upward. Stay the course. You will make it through to the other side.

Romans 15:13 "Now may the God of hope fill you with all joy and peace in believing, so that you will abound in hope by the power of the Holy Spirit." NASB

DAY 15

Pressing On

I mentioned earlier that we had two dogs die of cancer close together. I also mentioned that death is a very complex set of emotions for me, and by God's grace, I got through Dakota's death. A few months before his death, the Lord was teaching me a lesson about walking on water. This lesson started with the song "Oceans" from Hill Song. "You called me out upon the waters", is the first line to the song. I asked the Lord to show me what this meant.

Matthew 14:28-33 "Then Peter called to him, "Lord, if it's really you, tell me to come to you, walking on the water." "Yes, come," Jesus said. So Peter went over the side of the boat and walked on the water toward Jesus. But when he saw the strong wind and the waves, he was terrified and began to sink. "Save me, Lord!" he shouted. Jesus immediately reached out and grabbed him. "You have so little faith," Jesus said. "Why did you doubt me?" When they climbed back into the boat, the wind stopped. Then the disciples worshiped him. "You really are the Son of God!" they exclaimed." NLT

He spoke to me and said, "I'm teaching you to walk on water." I told Him I didn't understand. He continued, saying, "The miracle wasn't in walking on water. The miracle was keeping my eyes on Him during the storm." Then, in a vision, I saw myself walking on water. The water was raging in high waves. The sky was very black and lighting was shooting in all directions. Then, suddenly, I saw Jesus. Robed in white and there was peace in His face and calmness all around him.

And from the distance between us, what stood out was that amazing calmness. I could see nothing else but calmness.

Keeping my eyes on this sight, I stayed steady walking calmly towards Him. Arriving only inches from His face, out of the corner of my eye, I could once again see the reality in the storm's severity. It caused me to look all around and think, "Oh my Word! This storm is terrible." The vision ended. During my walking on the water, as I starred at Him, I didn't see the storm. It was like you either saw Him or you saw the storm, but you could not see both of them at the same time.

Getting an understanding of the scripture of how Peter sank when he took his eyes off the Lord, it was now making sense to me. Wondered filled me, of how the vision would have ended had I keep my eyes on Jesus. Pondering His words to me, "the miracle wasn't in walking on water. The miracle was keeping my eyes on Him during the storm." I knew I wanted to fully understand this lesson. Think about the worst storm you have ever witnessed or heard about. Can you imagine seeing Jesus during the storm and not seeing the storm at all because Jesus is so radiantly dressed in peace and calmness? But the moment you take your eyes off Him, you see the craziness of the storm. You can not, in no way, see crazy out of control at the same time as seeing the calmest radiant peace. The miracle really is keeping your eyes on Him during crazy times and not on the crazy.

Back to Dakota. The day had come that Dakota's suffering had to end. My husband, daughter and I arrived at the vet's office. We all loved this big fur boy. It overcame me with emotions of having to let him go, and facing another death, I felt faint-hearted. (God's word says, "You shall not faint"). The vet came into the room. Holding on to that big old St. Bernard head, I crying my eyes out. I then heard in my thoughts, "I taught you how to have a miracle. Keep your eyes on Me." Next, I saw Jesus, dressed in this glorious white. Arms wide open. The sun was shining all-around Him. Suddenly, Dakota leaped into His arms. For Jesus, it was as if they had been lifelong buddies. Jesus was hugging and loving on this enormous ball of happy fur, just like Dakota would greet us when we walked in the door. And at that minute the vet said, "He's gone".

I realized that as long as I kept my eyes on Jesus, I could see in the spirit realm our buddy crossing this world to that world, the earth realm to a heavenly realm. As Christians, we are always living out of two realms. The Kingdom of heaven (because Jesus is in us and all of who He is also is in us), and this realm of earth that is quickly fading away. We have a choice of where we will put our focus. The Lord told Peter he had little faith when he saw the storm. The reason is Peter caused his mind to be back to the earthen realm when he was in the Kingdom of heaven realm.

You, too, have a choice of where you want to live out of. You can keep looking at your circumstances from earth's perceptive or you can look at your circumstances from heaven's perspective. Seeing death from heaven's perceptive gave me a hope and a joy. Did I cry and feel grief? Yes, I did. For about three weeks, I felt the loss of our buddy boy. Every time I would feel that overwhelming sorrow, I would cause myself to grab hold of the truth. The truth that came from the true reality of the Kingdom of heaven realm. That truth was and is Dakota is enjoying Jesus, and Jesus is enjoying Dakota.

I would like for you to practice your miracle of taking your eyes off the storm and seeing Jesus. For some, this will come easy. For others, it will take practice. The Lord wants us to always have the mind of Christ. He wants us to live the miracle every day. Write about your miracle of being in the Kingdom of Heaven realm.

Romans 12:2 "And do not be conformed to this world, but be transformed by the renewing of your mind, that you may prove what is that good and acceptable and perfect will of God." NKJV

DAY 16

Repentance

Father, Your ways are so different from the way I think. I am finding the more I draw closer to You, the more I like Your ways. Although, I must confess, it is not always easy for me to fully understand. I feel caught up in confusion as I try to grasp understanding. I know confusion is not of You, so I ask that You help me take my thoughts captive to the obedience of Christ Jesus. Amen.

At this stage of my life, I believe the Lord is teaching me to I spend more time thinking about the sins of my thoughts. With all that is in me, I want to get this thing down right. After all, we have heard it said and can testify of the truth, that the battlefield is our mind. It is our stinking thinking that gets us in trouble with our faith.

When troubles seem to take over, do we honestly practice seeing Jesus? We can see a situation unfold right before our very eyes. We must deal with what we see. That is wisdom. How you deal with it is what the Lord is looking for in us. What are your thoughts following the discovery of a situation? Do any of your thoughts sound like these? "Oh Lord, did I handle that right? I should have done..." "What if nobody likes the way I handled this? It's going to cause issues, and I don't want to ruffle anyone's feathers." "This is my life, and I don't care what anyone thinks. I'm the one that has to live with it." "They will get what is coming to them." "Next time they will get a mouth full from me." "How dare they..."

According to these scriptures, these thoughts are sinful. Let us look at them.

Psalm 119:169 "Let my cry come before you, O Lord; give me understanding according to your word!" ESV

Romans 12:14 "Bless those who persecute you. Don't curse them; pray that God will bless them." NLT

Matthew 5:37 "Just say a simple, 'Yes, I will,' or 'No, I won't.' Anything beyond this is from the evil one." NLT

1 Corinthians 6:19 "Do you not know that your body is a temple of the Holy Spirit who is within you, whom you have [received as a gift] from God, and that you are not your own [property]?" AMP

Ephesians 4:31 "Let all bitterness and wrath and anger and clamor [perpetual animosity, resentment, strife, fault-finding] and slander be put away from you, along with every kind of malice [all spitefulness, verbal abuse, malevolence]." AMP

These are examples of what most of us have going on in our thought life. Scripture also says, "that as a man thinks" (my paraphrase). And here in lies the sin. As we think! Do you understand what is going on inside your heart when you are thinking negative thoughts? Does God have negative thoughts concerning you? Sometimes we believe the lie that He does, but never does He, who created us, think negatively about us. Scripture says we can grieve Him, cause Him to be angry, but never will He think negatively about us. No, not ever! (I just love that phrase.)

If we are to have the mind of Christ, how is it we have negative thoughts? Scripture tells us, "Casting down imaginations, and every high thing that exalteth itself against the knowledge of God, and bringing into captivity every thought to the obedience of Christ" 2 Corinthians 10:5 KJV. Hear me, the thoughts will come, but if we do not take them captive, what we do with those thoughts that cause us to sin.

I'm going back to the three second rule. When a negative thought enters your mind, you have three seconds to get rid of it before it hooks your soul. If it hooks you, then take responsibility for that thought. Give it to Christ and get rid of it.

Father, my thought on this matter has ahold of me. I made the choice to keep it instead of giving it over to You. Please help me release this thought over to You, and break its hold off me. Amen.

Our actions can result from the way we are thinking. We have to not only change our thinking, but change any actions that are the fruit of wrongful thoughts. Father, my actions towards _____ result from the thoughts I have held onto. I confess and repent of my actions and I want to walk in all Your ways. Help me, Lord, to let go of my negative thoughts and change my actions. Amen.

Every time that thought wants to take you on another journey, be quick to run to the Lord with it. Disable that thought quickly, through Jesus. You might have to go to Him every minute or a couple times a week, but don't become lazy about going back to Him with the thought. Get rid of it before it consumes you.

Father, it is me again. You must be tired of hearing from me over this thought. I am standing here again and will continue to come to You until I get the victory. Once again, I choose to take this thought captive and give the thought to You. Amen.

Taking a thought captive means that you want to think on right things. Godly things. Write out those godly thoughts in the space below.

_____
_____
_____
_____
_____
_____
_____

Colossians 3:17 "And whatsoever ye do, in word or in deed, do all in the name of the Lord Jesus, giving thanks to God the Father through him." ASV

DAY 17

Praying the Scriptures

Why is scripture good to use when praying? The scriptures are the inspired word of God. It is truth and nothing but the truth. The word speaks clearly what is the will of the Father. We are born into sin. Everything about us is contrary to the word of God until we accept Jesus Christ as Lord and Savior. After we accept the Lord as Savior, He does a work in our hearts. It is a purifying work. It is a restoration work..

Before Jesus, our life of sin is all we knew. Growing up and living in a world that is full of evil and sin can take away from what is good and what is truth, especially now. Truth is so watered down, it is becoming harder and harder for those who do not know Christ to accept Him as Savior. Sadly, in many churches, there isn't that defining line of what will make their life different from the world's way. Sin is just as ramped in the church as it is in the world.

BUT... if we turn to the Bible, the word of God, and use His own words for our promptings for prayer, we are then praying the perfect and acceptable will of God. My words can seem like futile attempts, but after praying with scripture, I can walk away feeling like I spoke the needs in my heart with accuracy. In the end, God knows our hearts and if we can not fully express what it is, we are praying to Him, He still fully understands what we are trying to say. What does it look like to you to become more like Christ or to even draw close to Him?

_____

_____

_____

_____

_____

_____

For me, it's starts with getting in His presence. Sometimes I put in worship instrumental music to create an atmosphere of peace. Sometimes it's going out to the cottage to get completely alone in the quiet. At other times, it is gathering together with like-minded believers to pray.

Revelation 21:3 "And I heard a loud voice from the throne saying, "Behold, the dwelling place of God is with man. He will dwell with them, and they will be his people, and God himself will be with them as their God." ESV

Come, Lord, and dwell with me and in me. As deep calls to deep, I call out to You to consume me with Your presence. Come and let this be a holy place and a holy moment. I am Your daughter, overwhelmed that You would even call me Your child. Bring me into You as You are in me. I love You, Jesus. Come and talk to me. Show me if there is anything holding me back from drawing closer to You and I will release it into Your hands. Let Your goodness wash over me and cover me with Your blood, cleansing all my sins away. Make me acceptable in Your sight, oh Lord, my rock and redeemer. Amen.

Write your prayer asking Jesus to bring His presence all around you and dwell with you.

_____

_____

_____

_____

_____

Psalm 51:10 "Create in me a clean heart, O God, and renew a right spirit within me." ESV

Matthew 5:8 "Blessed are the pure in heart, for they shall see God." ESV

Father, thank You for the work the Holy Spirit is doing in me. I feel the cleansing of my heart. And it makes me want more of Jesus. I long to see Jesus. I long to be with Him. He is my everything. Your love is a great love who can fully understand it. I thank you for allowing me to feel Your love. I know there is so much more to Your love and I want to comprehend it better than I do. You are so holy. So glorious. The earth has nothing to compare to You. Thank You.

Tell the Lord how much you love Him.

_____
_____
_____
_____
_____

Psalm 63:1-3 "O God, You are my God; Early will I seek You; My soul thirsts for You; My flesh longs for You In a dry and thirsty land where there is no water. So I have looked for You in the sanctuary, To see Your power and Your glory. Because Your lovingkindness is better than life, My lips shall praise You.

As the deer pants for water Jesus, I thirst and hungry for more of You. Everywhere I go, I search for You because I can not live without You. I know You are in everything, so please show Yourself to me. Your love and kindness gets me through this life. Never will I leave Your sweet presence. (I soak up this moment. I let Him have my thoughts. He deserves all of me. I am His!)

How bad do you want to fully know Him? Tell the Lord how much He means to you, because honestly, you can not live without Him.

_____
_____
_____
_____
_____
_____
_____

DAY 18

Trust and Faith

Back in the mid 90's, revival had broken out in Brownsville, Florida and Toronto, Canada. People received salvation, healing, and holy laughter. My friends were touched by this holy laughter and I wanted it too more than I can tell you. Growing up with abuse and carrying the weight of it long after I left home left my without laughter. I always longed to laugh. I never real found anything funny. I could smile, but not laugh.

One night two of my friends and I went to a meeting. The speaker preached on, "How Bad Do You Want It." People in the congregation were breaking our with laughter. I wanted it very badly. While preaching the speaker used this scripture, "A Gentile woman who lived there came to him, pleading, "Have mercy on me, O Lord, Son of David! For my daughter is possessed by a demon that torments her severely." But Jesus gave her no reply, not even a word. Then his disciples urged him to send her away. "Tell her to go away," they said. "She is bothering us with all her begging." Then Jesus said to the woman, "I was sent only to help God's lost sheep—the people of Israel." But she came and worshiped him, pleading again, "Lord, help me!" Jesus responded, "It isn't right to take food from the children and throw it to the dogs." She replied, "That's true, Lord, but even dogs are allowed to eat the scraps that fall beneath their masters' table." "Dear woman," Jesus said to her, "your faith is great. Your request is granted." And her daughter was instantly healed." NLT

When the alter call came the speaker spoke these words, "How bad do you want it? Bad enough to be called a dog?" I ran to the alter with so many other people. They all start laughing and I am bawling my heart out. The speaker put her hand on me and said, "I will not pray for you yet." My thought was, please don't reject me. After a long period of uncontrollable cry, I started to calm down. The speaker put her finger on my belly and said, "Father, now let it bible up inside her." Nothing happened as she continued on praying for others. In my heart I prayed, "Father I am not a dog that I should beg for this." Then I thought, wow, that was harsh. So I turned that thought around by adding, "But if I were a dog I would lick Your feet." And then it finally hit me. Deep gut laughter sprung up out of my belly.

I laughed for hours. It was one thirty in the mourning till we all got home. There was so much endorphins released from all that laughter that I felt intoxicated. I couldn't walk straight. My friends were holding me up. But the thing that I felt the most was this kind of liquid love pouring through my body with zingers of electricity. This sensation and laughter lasted 3 weeks. To finally know unspeakable joy! But to feel this love that I can not describe was not what I was expecting. I was full on God's love! It was Amazing! How about you? How bad do yo want it? How bad do you want Jesus to take you deeper? Bad enough to be called a dog? Bad enough to push through the tears of brokenness?

How about you? How badly do you want it? How badly do you want Jesus to take you deeper? Bad enough to be called a dog? Bad enough to push through the tears of brokenness?

Healing is coming. Restoration is coming. I know it seems like we are always playing the waiting game but truth be told, we have all had moments of triumph. You victory is just up a head of if you don't give up. Can you imagine how, this desperate girl was feeling when the speaker said, "I will Not pray for you yet?" It wasn't until days later as I pondered it all that I felt like the Lord was showing me that she saw how deeply wounded I was in my soul. I needed to cry as much of that pain away as I could. I needed to empty out the hurt so He could fill that space with joy. Joy felt so good.

What do you need to empty out of your soul so that He can fill you up with joy?

_____

_____

_____

What are you trusting the Lord to do in you?

_____

_____

_____

Do you have faith? Are you asking for faith? What does your faith look like?

_____

_____

_____

For two years I prayed and sought the holy laughter. Two years! Did God let me down? No, His timing was perfect. He was right on time. In the process He made me desperate for Him. He allowed my children to witness a sad mom turn into a joyful mom which spoke to their spirit and gave them desire for a move of God in their lives. Had it happened sooner they might not have understood. They would have been too young.

Trust, and have faith in God's timing while pressing onward and upward in Him. Remember faith the size of a mustard seed is all He is asking of you to have. He is also asking you to not give up but press in. You got this. The Holy Spirit is not going to let you go when you want it so badly. He is going to lead you to it.

Tell the Lord you trust Him.

_____

_____

_____

_____

_____

Numbers 6:24-26 "May the Lord bless you and protect you. May the Lord smile on you and be gracious to you. May the Lord show you his favor and give you his peace."

DAY 19

Praise Worship and Thanksgiving

We are going to work through Praise worship and thanksgiving little different. Please follow the directions at each phase. You might want to put on and worship instrumental to do activity. Get alone in a quiet place. Take a few deep breaths and get the sense that God is with you in the room at this moment now. Read out loud with confidence the scriptures and writings. Follow the directions for each phase. Take your time. This is not the time rush your way through. Make it your passion.

Praise

Stand and give Praise your all as you speak these words out loud.

Psalm 29:2 "Give unto the Lord the glory due unto his name; worship the Lord in the beauty of holiness." KJV

You are holy and righteous, Almighty God. There is nothing compared to you. The heavens declare the wonders of you Name. Praise the Lord. We praise You Holy Spirit for the miracles seen throughout all the earth. We Praise you Son of God and Son of Man, Our Rock and Salvation. You are the mighty warrior who has crushed the enemy. Victory belong to our God for ever and ever. Glory to the Name of the Lord! Hallelujah! Let everything that has breath praise the Lord. We exalt Your Name and shout it out that You are the Lord, the Savior of the World. Hallelujah to the One who is the Lamb of God and sits on the throne. Jesus, You who are faithful and true, we magnify Your Name. Let all the earth declare Jesus is Lord!

Continue on with your own words of praise. He is worthy of it all.

Worship

Bow down on your knees. Let tears flow if they are there. Be free to fully express yourself. Remember this moment is between You and Jesus.

Psalm 95:6 "O come, let us worship and bow down: let us kneel before the Lord our maker." KJV

I bow low before You, Lord. I worship You, the Holy One. My heart delights in Your holiness. For God you are full of splendor and majesty. So holy, Lord, You are so holy. My soul bows in the presence of the pure and holy God. The glory of the Lord shines down on me because of You tender mercies. I bathe my soul in your presence so that I can worship You in spirit and in truth. For who can stand in Your presence but he who has clean hands and a pure heart. You alone oh Lord have cleansed me and purified me through Your precious blood. Jesus you are worthy of my worship. Bless the Lord oh my soul and all that is in me, bless His holy and righteous Name. You pour blessings out on me and cause my heart to rejoice, how great You are. Tears well up within me because words are not enough to express Your goodness. I love You King Jesus. Continue on with your own words of loving worship. He is worthy of it all.

Thanksgiving

You may either stand or stay kneeling. And again be free in expressing yourself. Let nothing inhibit you when offering thanksgiving.

Psalm 26:7 "That I may proclaim with the voice of thanksgiving And declare all Your wonders." NASB

I will praise you with my whole heart. Before all creation, will I sing praise unto You, Almighty God. With my praises I thank You for thy lovingkindness and for Your truth. In my day of trouble, I cried out to You, oh Lord, and You answer me, giving me strength to make it through the day. My life is in Your hands and I feel safe. Thank you, Lord. You have forgiving all my sins and see them no more. How grateful I am for the new life I have in You. People have been place all around me by Your directions to encourage me and hold me up. When the doors seemed closed, You opened them and poured out blessing on my life. Happy am I, Lord my Provider. Thank you for knowing everything thing about me, for it was You who knit me together in my mother womb. My Lord, you wanted me. I say it again with a thankful heart, You wanted me. I belong to You and I wouldn't want it any other way. Thank You!

Continue on with your own words of thanksgiving. He is worthy of it all.

Was there one phrase of this exercise easier than another for you? Why?

_____
_____
_____
_____
_____
_____
_____

Can you feel a difference in the way you emotional feel after doing this exercise?

_____
_____
_____
_____
_____
_____
_____

Father, I want to thank you for taking the time to hear my brother/sister praise, worship and offer up thanksgiving to you. I pray that You have touched them in a way that they hunger to keep coming back to this day and doing over and over again. If my brother/ sister felt inadequate to speak praises, worship and thanksgiving, help them to keep pressing through. Let them not give up. Encourage them and let them know that you a pleased with them in Jesus' Name, Amen.

DAY 20

Proclaim and Declare

Psalm 18:2 NLT " The Lord is my rock, my fortress, and my savior; my God is my rock, in whom I find protection. He is my shield, the power that saves me, and my place of safety."

My God, I declare that You are the Solid Rock that never moves. You are my place of safety where I am secure. I declare, You are my Savior who has given me new life and that is an eternal life. I will never know death. Thank You, Lord. My soul is blessed and whole and nothing can change what You have done for me. Praise Your Great Name!

1 Thessalonians 5:21AMP " But test all things carefully [so you can recognize what is good]. Hold firmly to that which is good."

I declare Lord, You have given me wisdom to seek and understand that which is good. If it is not good then it is not what I want in my life. I seek the good and only the good, holding firmly to it with out wavering. Jesus, You are good. I hold firmly to Your ways. Thank You for showing me Your goodness that I may walking all of Your good ways!

2 Timothy 3:16 TLB "The whole Bible was given to us by inspiration from God and is useful to teach us what is true and to make us realize what is wrong in our lives; it straightens us out and helps us do what is right."

I declare that everything in the Bible is the truth and nothing but the truth. The Bible is good for it teaches me all Your ways, Lord, and shows me how to walk uprightly by following all Your commands. Lord, Your word helps me understand areas in my life that are not yielded to You so that I can surrender them to You and be free of these things that are not good. I love Your word. It gives me strength to live a righteous life and is my strength. Great is the Word of God!

Colossians 2:8 TLB "Don't let others spoil your faith and joy with their philosophies, their wrong and shallow answers built on men's thoughts and ideas, instead of on what Christ has said."

I declare that what Christ says is the truth and it is truth that I turn my ears to. When others speak from what they believe, I will seek the scriptures to find if it is the truth. I will not just take what man says and call it truth. Man has their own ideas and philosophies that often times do not line up with the Bible. My thoughts are built upon the Bible and the real truth that come from the Lord, God, Almighty! I am a truth seeker! I back everything up with the Word of God.

John 14:23 NLV "Jesus said, "The one who loves Me will obey My teaching. My Father will love him. We will come to him and live with him."

I declare that I have said yes to having Jesus live in my heart. I love Jesus. I will obey all the teachings of the Lord. He will give me understand so that I will know how to live rightly and follow Him. The Father loves me because I choose to run after Him. I choose to learn all His ways by reading the Bible everyday. I seek Him in prayer. I ask for wisdom and understanding. The Lord lives with me. I am not alone! I am loved by Jesus and my Heavenly Father! Praise God! Praise God, for His amazing love!

You do not have to rattle these proclamations and declaration off to move on. Say the first one. Say it again and again. Meditate on it. This will put it down deep on the inside of you. It will expand on the inside of your soul and you will feel life from just that one scripture and declaration. Then move on to the next one. It is a miracle in itself what the Word of God can do in our hearts and minds.

2 Peter 1:20-21 NLV "Understand this first: No part of the Holy Writings was ever made up by any man. No part of the Holy Writings came long ago because of what man wanted to write. But holy men who belonged to God spoke what the Holy Spirit told them."

God's word is the "Living Word." God's word "Gives Life." God's word "Sustains Life." God's Word is Alive! When we read the Word of God we are taking life into us through our eye gates. If we are reading the Word of God out loud, we are taking life in through our eye gates and ear gates, but our mouth is declaring that life into the atmosphere around us. Can you imagine the words you are reading out loud from the Bible, straight from the Holy Spirit, are floating around the room you are in and filling the room with life. Now people come into the room and they are changed by the atmosphere of the room.

Those words from the Bible being spoken out loud are like seeds. And the people are like soil. The seeds fall into the soil so that they can produce a sustaining, life giving crop. That is what it looks like when we look at this whole thing from the spirit realm or with spiritual eyes.

How did you feel after reading the scriptures and declaring them?

_____

_____

_____

_____

_____

God is for you! I am for you! We are waling this thing out together. You are doing a great job pushing through the hard stuff with the good stuff, the good Bible. God is working life in you and you are going to overcome. Say, "Amen"!

DAY 21

How Has Your Faith Grown

Testimonies are so important. When we tell others what God is doing in our lives, we build faith for them and we also increase our own faith. Did any of my stories increase your faith in the lord for you during this week?

_____

_____

_____

_____

_____

God wants us to see Him in everything around us so we remain encouraged by the life He gives in those things. Years ago people used this phrase, "So heavenly minded no earthly good." That phrase really bothered me. Why? Seeking the Lord on this matter, He showed me that it was not truth. The people who walked around saying this were people who couldn't deal with how closely some walked with the Lord. Using that statement could dumb them down in their faith. Making the individual feel like they were doing something wrong.

Not me! Let someone come and say it to me so I could reply back to them, "Why, thank you. What a compliment!" I want people to be jealous of my relationship with the Lord. If they are jealous then they will begin to go after all the things of God the way I had to to get this relationship with Jesus. God does want us, "so heavenly minded".

Are you thinking more about the Lord than you ever have?

Are you desiring more of God to consume your life?

This is where our Joy will be made complete. Don't you want to have complete joy? For several years I taught a woman's Bible study. Truth be told, there were a few ladies who really grasped the teachings and grew in faith. I became jealous for the faith they were gaining and that jealousy pushed me to go deeper even more for myself. This kind of jealousy is not an evil jealousy, it is a jealousy that causes a stirring, a hunger to have what they have.

We are all to encourage each other to come up higher, to desire more. Just like this Psalm 42:1 NKJV says, "As the deer pants for the water brooks, So pants my soul for You, O God."

Have you ever panted for water because you were that thirsty? Were you ever that hungry your gut felt like it was turning inside out? You got to have it right there, right then kind of moment?

This is pure growth for wanting more of Jesus in your life. This is going beyond a milk feed baby Christian, to a craving meat mature Christian. And here is thing, the Lord, is craving your love and worship of Him just as much! Even more than you could ever pant or crave Him. Oh, how He loves you my brother/sister. I desire for you to know this and never question it. His loved is solid as the very rock He calls Himself.

If this feels foreign to you then ask the Lord to show you. Father, There is always room in my heart to take on more of You. I could never get enough of You. I want to understand this deep level of love KayAnn is talking about. Will you opening up my understanding to grasp how high and how deep You love is? Can a person be so consumed in Your love that nothing else compares to it? I want to know. Lord, teach me, show me and open me up to the revelation of You love. I ask this in Jesus' Name. Amen!

Keep asking and keep seeking. Don't stop asking till He gives it. Remember: "How bad do you want it?" Even now as I write this to you, I want a fresh infilling myself. Take me even deeper still, Lord.

How have you grown this week?

_____
_____
_____
_____
_____
_____

What do you feel you need to work on the most as You Journey to the Pathway of Joy?

_____
_____
_____
_____
_____
_____

What one thing can you say was growth for you this week?

_____
_____
_____
_____
_____
_____

I am encouraged by you. You are pressing through. You haven't given up. I believe because you want to be healed and you want to see Jesus do a powerful work in you, that other can see and will say, "Wow, you are different. Tell me what you did to make this change in your life." You will then be able to share your testimony from the steps you took to to draw closer to Jesus. The Hope is that they will ask you to teach them or show them how they can draw closer to Jesus too and see the changes for their life also. You are a perfect example of the restoration God does in ones life!

DAY 22

For the Sake of Joy

So how do we immerse ourselves in true joy? By become an expert in God's goodness. Recognizing God's goodness is us seeing with our understanding that we've been given the Holy Spirit to fill us with life and to awaken our dead hearts. That is joy. We are adopted by the Father and He calls us His children. That is a joy that floods may soul. We are co-heirs with Jesus Christ receiving all His benefits. Joy, joy, joy, down in my heart. We've been given His Holy Word to know how to live so we are not wondering around aimlessly. We have purpose. The joy of having purpose. We can talk to the Father through the unlimited access of Jesus whenever and for however long. No time constrains. The abundant joy of never being alone. We can talk to the Father through the unlimited access of Jesus whenever and for however long. No time constrains. The abundant joy of never being alone.

Having hope causes us to think on the future outcome, through Jesus, during the darkest hours. That is true joy. That is our focus. You know that you know that Jesus is so good and how He has done so much already and He isn't done doing. You can put a smile on your face with that deep inner joy knowing He's with you and He has this all in control. And in time, His time, will you come fully through your valley of the shadow of death. With that inner deep joy you can say, "I will fear no evil for You, Lord are with me." Even if you can not see Him, but seeing with your understanding, you know He has always been there.

Joy is not loosing hope. Your hope is built on nothing less, then Who? Jesus blood and righteousness! NOTHING LESS! No, not ever! Be to Him what you are to Him. His joy, His love, His delight.

In my teen years my dad had a massive heart attack at the age of 37 years old. The doctors did five by passes. They told us these things don't last forever. My father had a second heart attack at the age of 45 again requiring another five by passes. Sadly, my dad passed away two weeks later. It was seven years between heart attacks. Seven years of me wondering what I was going to do if I ever lost my dad. At times afraid to be with him fearful of him dying infront of me. But the reality was that I wasted seven years of living and loving the life I had left with my dad. Seven wasted years.

Any the age of twenty-seven I had to babies that did not make full term. Olivia Elizabeth and Josiah Elisha. Almost 4 years later I would give birth to a healthy son. I thought once I had that son in my arms the pain of my grieving would go away. But it did not. Six more years it would take of carrying sadness and grief over what I did not have when I could have enjoyed what I did have. Six years of grief and pain.

It took be being exhausted from all the pain and suffering to cry out to the Father and say, I'm done carrying this pain. I can't do it any more. Please take it.

I can't find true joy Father, if I don't come to You, but I can initiate healing if I do come to You. Please, take my pain and start my healing. Bring me into the fullness of Your joy. I want to be whole in my soul and an example to others suffering. Oh what joy it is if we just immerse ourselves into Your presence and surrender all. Here Lord, I give You my pain and my brokenness. I give You all of me. Amen.

It's time to drink deeply, immersing ourselves in the gloriously satisfying gifts and promises of the Father. It's time to become experts in seeing and knowing all about His goodness.

If we give up on hope then we will never know the outcome of full JOY! Give Him everything today that is holding you back. Choose to just smile until He completes the work in you. If tears come then let them be tears of joy. Smile and thank Jesus for the work He is doing in you.

He is making you stronger yet softer. He is filling you with compassion. He is giving you the understanding of grace and mercy. And look! Oh, look and see! You are looking just like Him! You are beautiful! So beautiful!

Immerse yourself in Jesus, and tell Him of all His goodness that you know.

Now breathe in deep the breath of life that the Father has given you. Now breathe out. And breathe in again thanking Hime for the breath of life that is in your lungs. And breathe out.

Romans 8:28 ESV "And we know that for those who love God all things work together for good, for those who are called according to his purpose."

Proverbs 3:5 ESV "Trust in the Lord with all your heart, and do not lean on your own understanding."

1 Peter 5:7 AMP "casting all your cares [all your anxieties, all your worries, and all your concerns, once and for all] on Him, for He cares about you [with deepest affection, and watches over you very carefully]."

Can you say, "Thank You, Jesus"?

DAY 23

Repentance

When life comes at you with one situation after another, you begin to even wonder if God is there. Does God even care about you anymore? Did you commit a sin so great that you made Him mad, so now you are being punished?

In moments like these, have you considered that opposite? Maybe the Lord is trying to show you how big He is. Our natural way of thinking is, "If God were there, then why isn't He doing something?" But what if the Lord was saying, Wait till they see all that I'm going to do in this!" We can easily see the Lord moving when things come up one at a time and we go off praising the Lord telling everyone what God did. It is a different story when everything is coming at us at one time and we feel like we can't breathe. Then we begin to accuse God of abandoning us.

Back in the nineties, David Wilkerson wrote an article titled, "Accusing God of Child Neglect." That article changed my thoughts from ever thinking the Lord was not with me. When we blame the Lord for anything we are facing... if you re going through a difficult situation... been diagnosed with an illness... facing financial lack... What we are really saying when we cry out with these words, "God where are You?" is accusing God of Child neglect!

That was profound to me. I love the Lord so much that I could never accuse Him of child neglect, but I did. My murmuring, whining, my woe is me reactions was accusing God of child neglect. Honestly, that article was a spiritual awakening for me as I sat there weeping from the pit of my stomach.

There is another thing that happens in times like these. It starts off with a worship songs first line, "I have made You too small in my eyes. Lord, forgive me." He is a BIG God. He is a big Father.

Jeremiah 29:11 ESV "For I know the plans I have for you, declares the Lord, plans for welfare and not for evil, to give you a future and a hope."

The Father has you. You are not going to slip from His hands. He did not create you to watch you suffer and then leave you for the day of torture. You are His delight. He is a good Father.

Philippians 4:19 ESV "And my God will supply every need of yours according to his riches in glory in Chri.st Jesus."

Have you ever made Him too small in your eyes? Have you ever accused the Lord of child neglect? We all have at some point. This is your time to repent and tell the Lord how sorry you are. This is the time to make He big again in your eyes and see Him as a good father who has everything under control. Tell Him how sorry you are for thinking less of him then what He really is,

_____
_____
_____
_____
_____
_____

Now tell Him what a good Father He is.

_____
_____
_____
_____
_____
_____

Telling the Lord how good He is like like taking "good" medicine for your soul. It will break off the negative thinking and lighten the heavy load hanging on your soul. This conversation is speaking truth. You soul needs truth instead of the lies we feed it when we are discouraged.

My brother/sister I want to see you be as free as you can possible be. Free from discouragement, especially free from thinking that the Father is not for you. He is working all things out. You are going to be amazed at the end of this just how much control He had in it.

Keep repenting of anything that comes to you during anytime of the day or night. I have been at friend's homes when I thought comes to me. I don't wait I act like I have to go to the bathroom and I repent right there. I want to get rid of thing as quickly as I can so that I do not bog my soul down with any for of darkness. Repentance will keep you close to the heart of your heavenly Father.

One dat extremely soon, we will be here no more. We will be with Him for He is coming for a pure and spotless Bride to take us home. We will never have to repent again for we will see Him and know Him in HIs fullness and HIs greatness.

I often think when we go to heaven that I will wrap my arms around the neck of Jesus and I won't let go. How could I? I am longing and have been waiting for this day literally my whole life. I can not wait to get there and be with the Lord forever. To look into His face and see His eyes that are so full of love. Heaven a place that is so perfectly balanced in every single thing, and yet for us it will feel like the greatest extreme of everything good any one person could ever witness.

It will happen soon. So do not give up. Keep press in in take hold of the hope keeping that your focus from now till that day. You have grown so much. I'm proud of you!

Philippians 3:12 ESV "Not that I have already obtained this or am already perfect, but I press on to make it my own, because Christ Jesus has made me his own."

DAY 24

Praying the Scriptures

One thing that I have not touched on yet is journaling. It is the reason for writing this book. When being diagnosed with Hashimoto thyroiditis, I created a journal to keep track of my symptoms. This way, I'd know if I was doing too much and needed to slow down. Other journals I use include journals for recording God's conversations, a dream journal, a scripture journal for when a revelation of the scriptures comes to me, and a prayer journal.

My prayer journal records request, scripture that are relevant to the request, so I'm praying God's Word right into the request. I also leave space in-between each request to record the answers when they come in. This has been such a meaningful way to watch God move and answer prayers. I tell you, when you see the answers to your prayers, it is praiseworthy, and uplifting. It causes you to want to pray more for the needs of others. Create your own prayer journal or purchase prompting prayer journals that have a wonderful layout on each page for you.

I want to start with the Lord's prayer:

Matthew 6:9-13 ESV "Pray then like this: "Our Father in heaven, hallowed be your name. Your kingdom come, your will be done, on earth as it is in heaven. Give us this day our daily bread, and forgive us our debts, as we also have forgiven our debtors. And lead us not into temptation, but deliver us from evil." There was a season I was into praying this every day. When I was first prompted to pray this, it felt strange to say, "Our, us, we," because it was me praying alone by myself.

Then God! Knowing my thoughts, He gave me the answer through a sermon that taught a wonderful answer. When we pray this prayer, even if we are alone while praying it, we are to including everyone we know who believe in Jesus Christ as Lord. We are asking for the needs to be met for ourselves and for our other brothers and sisters whom we have met and the ones we have not met. We are praying in unity for the whole church, the Bride of Christ.

How beautiful is that? Christ Jesus wrote out the entire prayer for you. You don't have to hunt for the entire community of believer's prayer needs, God covers it all in this prayer. The prayer Jesus taught the disciples and us to prayer. That makes it a perfect prayer.

There are other scriptures in the Bible that give us directions on how to pray.

Luke 5:15-16 AMP "But the news about Him was spreading farther, and large crowds kept gathering to hear Him and to be healed of their illnesses. But Jesus Himself would often slip away to the wilderness and pray [in seclusion]." This scripture speaks of the importance of getting alone to pray. In the last home we owned, I used a bedroom to create a prayer room. I enjoyed that room, decorating it with things that delighted me. It was bright and happy. When I would go into that room, I could feel the peace of God in there. We currently now live in a tiny house. We purchased a shed we call the "Hatching Nest." This is my art studio, guest house, and most importantly, the prayer room. I feel the same about it that I did my first prayer room. Some people do not have the space to make a prayer room.

Here is my suggestion. Create a board that you can hang on the inside of a closet door. Put a scripture on it that inspires you. Post prayer needs, or pictures of those you're praying for. You can also make a banner of sorts that speaks of this place being your prayer space. When it is time for prayer, go to this place and open the door and let that space close you in somewhat so that it feels like a shelter, a place of seclusion.

Luke 11:9-10 NLT "And so I tell you, keep on asking, and you will receive what you ask for. Keep on seeking, and you will find. Keep on knocking, and the door will be opened to you. For everyone who asks, receives. Everyone who seeks, finds. And to everyone who knocks, the door will be opened." This scripture was vital to me in the early days of prayer. When I was learning to pray I felt like I just keep asking for the same things over and over. I didn't know to pray the scriptures and I don't know what other words to use. When this scripture appeared in my reading it calmed my mind down. I just asked over and over and over again. God meets us at all stages of our lives and He knows our every thought. Our prayers just need to be sincere and heart felt. We are not praying to say, "Yep, got my pray time in," We are praying to meet needs and spend time fellowshipping with a wonderful Holy God.

We are all at different stages of our Christian walk. For some you will find this prayer section helpful and for others you will have already known this information. Either way, let us all be encouraged to keep walking in communion with the Lord and continue growing and mature as the scripture say we should. For me, it was during those most difficult times that I needed to hear it again. Not knowing why, it seems when those overwhelming times in living life that we forget. We lose track of our routines as we take time to grieve. Having someone tell us how to get back on track helps us to move forward.

What have you found most helpful in praying the scriptures today?

_____
_____
_____
_____
_____

Father God, the truth is for some of Your children, they may need a fresh new way to approach prayer. I pray that the suggestion that are spoken of in this reading would encourage and bring hope to their prayer life. As they walk forward in their prayer life, I ask that you take them deeper in fellowship with You. Let their prayer time become a two-way conversation with You. But during those times when no words are adequate, I pray they know the power behind their prayers of tears, as Charles Spurgeon called them, "liquid prayers." In Jesus' Name. Amen!

Romans 8:26-27 NLT "And the Holy Spirit helps us in our weakness. For example, we don't know what God wants us to pray for. But the Holy Spirit prays for us with groanings that cannot be expressed in words."

DAY 25

Trust and Faith

The next phase of our journey was working through bankruptcy. That would take five years to complete. We would have to make assigned payments to our debtors until the time was up. It was required of us to fill out a sheet on our bills and debts. The sheet was sent into the lawyer. He took that information and put it on the hard copy that would be filed with the bankruptcy court. After we filled in all our debt information we learned the monthly court payment and we felt it was high. I was grieved about this amount. The lawyer asked us to double check everything before he finalized it.

Looking at the hard copy, we saw that it had a spot for tithing that was not on the first paper we were giving. We have a strong conviction on tithing no matter what our finances look like. Adjusting that bit of information finished what was required of us and we sent it back to the lawyer. Within seconds he was calling us. "Mr. and Mrs. Engleman you can not add tithing to this form unless you can provide proof that you tithe." Responding back that we can, he explained, "That changes everything in a big way. Your payment will drop substantially." I began to cry. He asked, "Why would you tithe such an amount of money?" Answering his question with, "The scripture says to bring your tithe into the storehouse. If we don't tithe churches won't exist. That is how they pay bills, their staff and purchase learning materials for kids programs and adult classes. It is how they help those that come in for finical need."

That hard copy saw tithing as a weekly bill. A court system that somewhere along the line valued those who were committed to giving to God what belonged to God. For the first time through this whole ordeal the tears I cried were tears of joy and praised. God was getting glory and honor right there. It became a witness to our lawyer.

There were other miracles that took place. At the time of bankruptcy we were near the end of a car lease. When it came time to hand the leased car in we were given approval to lease another car. They told us we were the first they ever saw to get approval to make that kind of purchase. For years we talked about moving to a quiet location. An opportunity presented itself, but if we sold our house the courts would take all that we made on the sale of our house leaving us with nothing to use as a down payment for our new house. It was explained to us that we could rent our property until the bankruptcy was over in two years. The Lord gave us a renter almost on the spot.

While all this was going on these pass three years I held onto the promise I felt the Lord put in my heart that we would not complete the full five years of the bankruptcy. Then the day came to turn in our leased car. They said to us, "You know looking over everything if you can come up with X-amount of dollars we can end your bankruptcy early." We had been able to save enough money to pay that amount. We ended the bankruptcy a year early! God kept His promise.

Praise God for his faithfulness! We sold our home and made more for it than we thought we would. We built a home, own a truck and car and we are completely debt free to this day. That bankruptcy taught us to live with out credit cards and pay cash for everything. And it taught us what it is like to owe no man. We are FREE!

I have told the Lord, "Thank You for what I got out of this, BUT... I will also thank You to never take us through something like that again." I still can not help but to see all that I have learned walking through the bankruptcy. I can see the many miracles of provision, and yet, I willing acknowledge that I am absolutely sure that there is much the Lord did that I can not see. For that reason, I am humbled by His overwhelming goodness.

He had giving me faith in the midst of the storm so that I could keep my focus on Him. My trust has become more solid than I ever thought it would be. And it is through difficulties like this that I could have been angry and walked away from the Lord, but I didn't. I decided long ago that no matter what He was God and I was not. I would never leave Him or forsake Him. He will always be my God, especial when

I don't understand or could not make sense of the mess. If I hold on to that, one day I will see and witness His glory shine through my darkness. And it did!

Tell me a story about about His glory shining thorough for you. I don't care how small or how big, testify to me how God has moved for you.

_____
_____
_____
_____
_____
_____
_____
_____
_____
_____
_____

It is always good to talk of the things you can remember that God has done for you. I have just as many, if not more, wonderful stories of God's goodness in my life than the bad and overwhelming. It's just that it is many times difficult to see the good during the bad. I tell you, if you will make a written inventory of everything the Lord has done for you that you can think of, then when life hits hard, you get that list out and you read it over and over and over. Don't you ever forget how your trust and faith have been built by the goodness of God. He will not fail you now. You are too close to making. You are going to get through this. I promise you because my promise is backed by His Word.

Philippians 1:6 AMP "I am convinced and confident of this very thing, that He who has begun a good work in you will [continue to] perfect and complete it until the day of Christ Jesus [the time of His return]."

DAY 26

Praise, Worship, and Thanksgiving

Father God, I offer up praises to Your great name. What a wonderful joy I feel when I get to see You move on my behalf and the behalf of others. Though often times it is hard to understand why the difficulties, You have always shown Yourself to be faithful. You have turned the most difficult impossibilities making them possible because all things are possible with You. It is all because of Your great love for us. Again, another thing that is hard to comprehend and put into words how thankful we are for Your love shown to us. Jesus, with gratitude we thank You for seen and unseen ways You have cared for us in all areas of our lives. We thank You that we are important to You. Amen!

Can you imagine this: you are in a room with one hundred people. No one touching each other. The lights go out. There are no widows for any type of light to come in. It is utter complete darkness. Each person in the room with you has a candle including yourself. But you are the only one who has a means to light that candle. As long as you choose to not light that candle the room will always remain in darkness. After a long period of time and complete darkness you decide you had enough of the darkness and you light your candle. That single flame of light is enough to show you how close some people were standing next to you. You may be able to tell whether there were females or males around you but there is still not enough light to make out their faces. Most amazingly, that one flame pushed the deep darkness away from in front of you. Light pushes darkness away! NO light, brings darkness in like a flood.

You begin to see how your one flame helped you to see in front of you. But what if you lit the candle of a few people around you? So you ask them to hold up their candles and you light theirs with yours. Now you can see details of the surrounding faces. Shadows are cast onto the walls from creating more light, but there are still many who have not had their candles lit, so you decide you want all the darkness gone and for everyone to be fully in the light. Everyone's candles are now lit, glowing with a flame of light. They engulf the room with light. No more darkness. No more shadows. The light broke through the darkness and sent it fleeing in every direction.

Going through difficulties that put me in the darkest place feeling hopeless with no end in sight. But one day, that light that Jesus put in my heart began to shine again. And He fanned into flame the flicker that seemed like it was going out. I could see again. All darkness was pushed back. But It wasn't until I decided to light the candles of those around me that I saw a greater hope and purpose for all that I had gone through. It was for you! And for the person that you share this Pathway to Joy journal with. A person who also is needing hope and whose flame is flickering. Then you will be lighting their candle and hopefully they will light someone else candle.

This whole world will be lit with hope. The only Hope that Christ gives. A hope that changes lives. There has been a process and a journey to walk this pathway to joy. But oh the joy if we do not give in nor give up. The next time something else comes your way you will use the steps in this prompting journal to once again walk forward and upward so that you do not get lost in the grief and guilt of difficulty. And as surely as Christ will rescue you through this one, He will rescue you again, and you will have gained faith, grow in trust and mature as a Christ follower. You're a solider now in the Army of the living God. He has used all the circumstance to equip you for the next steps of your amazing journey.

I've said it before and I'll say it again, I am so proud of you for pressing in and not giving up. I know how hard it has been for you. But I also know how the Lord was with you through it all. I can't wait to see and hear how He will use all that you learned from this experience. If I don't ever get to meet you personally this side of heaven, I sure will meet you on that side of heaven. You're my brother/sister. Our Heavenly Father is a family man (so to speak). When He says on that day that is upon us any moment now, "Son go get your Bride," we will all be at the celebration of the Lamb and embracing each other as one big happy family and I will hear all about how Jesus used you on the earth. I can not wait! Come, Lord Jesus, come. The Spirit and the Bride say come!

Who can you share this Pathway to Joy with?

_____

_____

_____

_____

Your testimony it so valuable to share with others. It will give people hope and that is what people are looking for. They want to know that if someone made it through their difficulties, then maybe they can too. What would you tell others of how this journey helped you? How has God made Himself real to you?

_____

_____

_____

_____

_____

_____

The words to an old hymn come to mind right now... "When we all get to heaven what a day of rejoicing that will be, When we all see Jesus we will sing and shout the victory!" My brother/sister, yes we will. I can not wait. I am so very excited as each day passes that it is that much sooner. We don't have to wait for that time to sing and shout the victory. Do it now! While the world is looking outrageous with their blatant acts of sin, you look like a sports fan screaming for team Jesus. He is so worth the cheer and happy dance. Amen? Amen!

Isaiah 12:2 MSG "Yes, indeed—God is my salvation, I trust, I won't be afraid.God—yes God!—is my strength and song, best of all, my salvation!"

DAY 27

Proclaim and Declares

You are a soldier in God's army. The Holy Spirit has been equipping you during this season. Your difficulties have not gone to waste. It has been making you stronger yet gentle. You have been learning how to use the Sword of the Spirit, which is the Word of God, to hold your ground. You have been declaring and proclaiming that God will do what He said He is going to do. Faith has been increasing. Trust has been growing. Your moment is upon you for Kingdom living!

Stand immovable: 1Corinthains 15:58 NLT "So, my dear brothers and sisters, be strong and immovable. Always work enthusiastically for the Lord, for you know that nothing you do for the Lord is ever useless."

Keep standing: Ephesians 6:13 NLT "Therefore, put on every piece of God's armor so you will be able to resist the enemy in the time of evil. Then after the battle you will still be standing firm.

When you done all you know to do, stand immovable! You have the Victor living you! The difficulties we go through are not to show us how weak we are but to show us how strong we have become. It is the Lord who builds strength in us. It is for such as time as this that the Lord has been preparing you. He was reducing the amount of flesh and increasing the spiritual side of you. He has building courage in you to with stand the fear the enemy has been holding you back with. There

Lord also brought you to your knees so that you can see that it is He who fights your battles.

Tell the Lord you will remain faithful.

_____

_____

_____

_____

_____

As long you hold your ground, keep your heart pure through repentance, speak God's Word into your circumstances, cast down every vain imagine that sets itself up against the Word of God, then you are doing all you know to do. When we do our part we give God the good stuff to be able to fight our battles. This is what Pathways to Joy is all about. It is just another tool for you to walk in victory.

When we do all that scripture instructs us to do we will always get the victory. We will never be overcome. God's Word is true, it is yes and Amen. I'll say it again, shout it out, 'My God has given me the victory!" The Lord will do for you what He has done for David in battle. You have the Victory! He will do for you what He did for Paul when he was in prison, break those chains! When we obey His instructions like Deborah, we will over take the enemy. When we press in, no matter what anyone thinks, we will get our healing just like the woman with the issue of blood. When we become like children and come to Him, and if anyone tries to hinder that, He will rebuke them just like He did to His disciples. You are in a win-win situation.

Declare your victory!

_____

_____

_____

_____

_____

Father God, You have a good plan for my brother/sister that WILL come to past. No matter what part of the process they are walking through, it is certain that it will have an end. I pray that you help my brother/sister to keep their eyes on You and the prize for which they are journeying too. Love never fails. I ask that this journey shows them the deep love that You have for them. Let Your love full them with hope and joy, building strength and courage as they put their total faith in You. Thank you for never leaving them alone but staying right by their side. In Jesus' Name. Amen.

What do you need to ask the Lord for in this moment?

_____

_____

_____

_____

_____

_____

Salvation is yours through Jesus Christ. Is blood is your protection and covering causing you to be dressed is garments of righteousness. Spending time in the Word, praying is how you clothe yourself in the armor of the Lord. He has given Hs angels charge over you and they surround you like a hedge of protection. The holy spirit is your rear guard yet He leads you. With all this going on it cause one to wonder how on earth does the devil ever attack and cause damage? I just want to say it one more time that we have a responsibility to surround our will, resist the devil, and keep all doors closed that would be a way for him to come in.

Through you journey to Pathways to Joy, what doors have you had to close?

_____

_____

_____

_____

_____

_____

DAY 28

My, How Your Faith has Grown!

My brother/sister, life is difficult as you well know, but we have the promises of God that He will bring us through it all. You are not forsaken; you are loved. My earthly father went to heaven when I was only twenty-two. Although I missed my dad greatly, I knew deep in my soul I was not fatherless.

You and me, we have the same great and amazing Father. That is why I can testify to that you are going to make it. Our Father treats all his children the same. I feel in my spirit that you understand that more now than you ever did. I want you to remember that this journey will present you with more difficult times and it always seems to come right before we get a kind of spiritual promotion. Joyce Meyer has said, "New level, new devil."

We know that God's Word says that we are going from glory to glory. We see it as hard, but the Lord sees it as glory. He never views things the way we do because He knows the end results. I hope that you have grown in glory and that you can see future situations as glory climbing; going from glory to glory!

To be honest with you, I did not see the "from glory to glory" while going through all the things I was facing to which I shared with you. I wished I could have. Had I been able to, I would have let the peace of God that guards our hearts keep me from going into a deep depression. That is a big reason for this book. I don't want to see you make the same mistakes that I did. I want to see you keep your peace. Hold fast to it. It will determine how you emotionally do in the end.

Tell the Lord that you want Him to guard your heart.

_____

_____

_____

_____

_____

I'm hoping it was enough of a lesson for me to carry the peace of God in my heart from this day forward. I can envision myself walking around with a huge smile on my face at all times. People are walking past me and saying, "What is there to smile about?" With that big old smile, I will answer, "Because I am walking through glory." Give them something to talk about and think about that is contrary to their thinking. Show them through your presence and body language that you don't have to act the way the world acts.

We are a new creation, and old things have passed away. Dress yourselves in the new. Play the part. It is show time to the rest of the world of how we are to act if you fully trust Jesus. I'm not saying you won't have those moments, but I'm encouraging you to not let those moments over take you. Live on purpose to the belief that God is who He says He is and does what He says He will do. There is nothing less than that to live by.

You can do it! You can be a walking testimony of life to a lost and dying world who needs to see a faithful servant of Jesus living the life of security because we have nothing to worry about. God has everything under control. Do you see others living that way? Can you be that person to a hopeless people? Can you share your confidence in Jesus by living like the victory has already been handed over to you?

I believe you can. I believe you will not let that devil have one more second of your life. You will not give that devil any more power over you, by feeling and acting defeated. That is not who you are! Who are You? Answer: A Child of the Lord God almighty! Does He lose battles? Never! Are you defeated ever? No! Not ever!

I really am proud of you. This life in Jesus takes courage, but oh the rewards.

Ask the Lord for His power to hold you up to do the things you never thought possible.

_____

_____

_____

_____

_____

With hope, tell the Lord what you like to see come out of your difficult time so that you know the victor's reward.

_____

_____

_____

_____

_____

_____

_____

_____

_____

Father God, I pray for the courage of my brother/sister to be found in You. That they are brave to stand and be immovable in their faith and trust in Jesus. When we ask Father, You give us what we need. Help my brother/sister be strong while we are standing in the last days upon the earth. As long as we are still here, we have got to tell others You are faithful and that Jesus died to save us. Help us to have the courage and the strength to share salvation with others. Let us see the souls needing salvation as our brothers and sister and have that mind set that, "We can not lose our family to damnation." Work in our heart a passion for seeing a lost and dying world come to know eternal life. Amen.

I want to thank you for walking with me through Pathway to Joy. These are steps I took to overcome the difficult circumstance in my own life. I am aware that we all have different difficulties, but the common denominator to getting through is the same for those in Christ Jesus.

Taking the time to understand how we got here. Was it sin or disobedience, insecurities, lack of trust, self-pity, not seeking God for our steps and making our own decisions are some of things can cause difficulties in our life. Asking that question How did I get here is a way to examine your heart and motives. Are they out of alignment of God's will?

Repentance is key to getting right with the Lord. It shows humility, surrender and submission to NOT our will but His will. Just like Jesus in the garden when it was time for His crucifixion, "Not my will be down but Father Your will be done."

Prayer and Scripture will beep you close to the heart of God by submitting your soul to His presence. Prayer is communing with the Lord. It is a conversation that builds relationship. While scripture strengthens our faith. Hebrews tells us faith comes by hearing the word of God. Read the word out loud and let your soul hear it.

Trust and faith is vital to our relationship with the Lord. Hebrews tells us that it is impossible to to please God without faith. If we have faith in God then surely we are trusting Him. If He is the only one who can save us from our circumstances then it seem that we will need trust and faith to believe God will do what He said He is going to do.

Praise, worshiping, and thanksgiving build hope for breakthrough. It tells that, "God I believe every word You spoke concern me. That I'm not staying in this place and You will make away through this valley of death." Even if you don't feel like, praise, worship, and thank Him anyway. We don't live by by sight. We live by faith. God is going to do what He said He will do. In this truth offer Him it all.

Proclaim and declare the word of God out loud and in the truth. This is all based on God's Word which it truth. You are building up your inner man. You are saying what you choose to believe. It causes you to stand firm immovable.

Finally, stand back and ask your self periodically if your are making improvements. You will have peeks and valleys. Taking an inventory of your spiritual growth. You need to recognize any spiritual growth and celebrate your growth. Encourage yourself. Get others involved with your growth and to celebrate with you.

Your amazing! Thank you for taking the walk in Pathways to Joy. It was exciting to be apart of the work God is doing in you.

Under His Mantle of Mercy,
KayAnn Engleman

ABOUT THE AUTHOR

KayAnn Engleman and her husband are the parents of three children and nine grandchildren. She is a certified Master Mental Health Coach specializing in grief and loss. KayAnn holds weekend encounter retreats for women twice a year. She and her team have seen healings, miracles, and deliverances during the encounter weekends. She is gifted in teaching and the prophecy. KayAnn has been invited as a guest speaker for churches, conferences, and special events.

KayAnn has a passion and dedication to honor the Lord in everything she does. She founded Mantle of Mercy Ministries in 2002. With the help of her team members, many people have experienced an encounter with the Lord that brought healing and renewed faith in Jesus. KayAnn's hope is that those discovering Pathways to Joy will also be impacted in their faith and find a renewed life in Jesus. KayAnn is authentic in her passion to see more people walk in healing and grow deeper in their relationship with Jesus. "Everyone has a story of a difficult time in their life. I feel called to help people find the perfect ending to their story through the Holy Spirit."

www.ingramcontent.com/pod-product-compliance
Lightning Source LLC
Chambersburg PA
CBHW020327130626
46549CB00003B/1062